the breath

Also by Vessantara:
Meeting the Buddhas
Tales of Freedom
The Mandala of the Five Buddhas
The Vajra and Bell
Females Deities in Buddhism

the art of meditation

the breath

vessantara

Windhorse Publications

Published by
Windhorse Publications Ltd
11 Park Road
Birmingham
B13 8AB
UK
email: info@windhorsepublications.com
web: www.windhorsepublications.com

The right of Vessantara to be identified as
the author of this work has been asserted by him in
accordance with the Copyright, Designs and Patents Act 1988

Cover design Satyadarshin
Printed by Gopsons Papers Ltd, India

British Library Cataloguing in Publication Data:
A catalogue record for this book is available from the British Library

ISBN-10: 1 899579 69 9
ISBN-13: 978 1 899579 69 3

the art of meditation series

Meditation is a skill, a tool, an art. It offers us many ways into peace, happiness, joy, self-knowledge, compassion, and wisdom. There are a multitude of Buddhist meditation practices. While many books try to describe them all together, each book in this series will provide a more intensive look at an individual meditation.

At the core of each book will be a practical introduction to the meditation under consideration. In the case of many of the titles, there will also be reference to a broader applicability of awareness of the breath, the development of positive emotions, and awareness of the body.

There are several levels planned for this series.

The introductory level will include:
- The breath: the mindfulness of breathing
- The heart: the mettā bhāvanā (loving-kindness)
- The body: body scans and walking meditation

Further levels may include:
- The brahma vihāras ('sublime abodes')
- Satipaṭṭhāna or Ānāpānasati
- Pure awareness
- The six element practice
- Visualization

— the art of meditation is the art of life —

contents

about the author

Vessantara started breathing in London in 1950. Interested in Buddhism since his teens, he first had direct contact with Buddhists in 1971. In 1974 he became a member of the Western Buddhist Order and was given his Buddhist name, which means 'universe within'. He has a particular interest in Tibetan Buddhism and has had several Tibetan teachers.

He holds an MA in English from Cambridge University and a professional social work qualification. He is the author of seven books, including *Meeting the Buddhas* and *Tales of Freedom*, and has led retreats and workshops in Europe, the USA, India, and Australasia.

These days he divides his time between periods of intensive meditation, writing, leading retreats and aiding the development of several Buddhist centres. He also acts as a mentor to people joining the Western Buddhist Order. When not travelling he is based in Cambridge, England.

acknowledgements

Writing about the breath inevitably makes you see the world in terms of giving and receiving, taking in and giving out. So, before we start, I want to thank all those whose teaching, help, and support has enabled me to pour out these ideas about the breath onto paper.

Vajradaka first taught me to meditate on the breath, and I have never forgotten those early classes. Sangharakshita's seminar on Chih-I's text *Dhyana for Beginners* was seminal for my whole understanding and practice of the meditation. I've also really appreciated my many discussions with Kamalashila, which have stimulated my thinking about meditation in general. More recently, Larry Rosenberg's book *Breath by Breath* (see Further Reading for details) widened my horizons about the practice. I'm also grateful to Karunavira for his teaching on a retreat in Sussex earlier this year.

However, learning is like breathing: sometimes we notice ourselves taking in air, but a lot of the time it happens without our being aware of it. So those are just some influences that particularly come to mind, and there have been many others. This book is a distillation of my experience over many years: sitting in on classes where this meditation was taught, and practising it myself in daily life and on meditation retreats, as well as my own teaching. I'm particularly grateful to all those I have taught, whose questions and accounts of their own experience have enriched my understanding.

In addition I've drawn on all the sources mentioned in the Further Reading section, plus many other books over the years. I was particularly helped by an unpublished manuscript on breath meditation by Virachitta, as well as notes produced by Tejananda and other meditation teachers at Vajraloka Buddhist Meditation Centre in Wales.

Once I started writing, I had some very helpful readers' reports on the first draft. Publishers' readers remain anonymous, so I can't thank them by name. As ever, my editor Jnanasiddhi has been a sensitive and supportive reader, suggesting ways of breathing life into bits of the text that were dull and dreary, and keeping me on track through the whole process of writing. As well as her I want to thank all the very dedicated staff at Windhorse Publications, with whom I always enjoy working.

The final draft was written on retreat at the Hermitage of the Awakened Heart in Snowdonia. I'm grateful to all those who live and work here for giving me such good conditions in which to complete the book.

Lastly, Vijayamala read an early draft, made many useful comments, encouraged me, and gave me a very supportive environment in which to write. I am deeply grateful.

Vessantara
North Wales
12 December 2004

introduction

why meditate on the breath?

I was first taught to meditate on the breath in January 1973 at a small Buddhist centre converted from a piano factory in a down-at-heel part of North London. I had already been meditating, on and off, for a few years. I went along because the Buddhist centre I had previously been attending was in the wilds of Scotland, hundreds of miles from London where I was training to be a social worker. I wanted to team up with some other meditators a bit closer to home, so I found out about the place in North London and went along to the introductory meditation class. Although I knew a bit about meditation, this was the first time I had been taught to use my breath as the focus. The meditation was explained in four stages, a method we shall learn in Chapter 2. The introduction was basic and simple, and within twenty minutes I was trying out the meditation for myself.

It would be nice to report that I fell in love with this meditation on that first night, had an amazing experience, and lived with it happily ever after. But it wasn't like that kind of story-book romance. If it was a story it would be more like the one in which you fall in love with the wrong person, it doesn't work out, but you have a faithful friend who is always there for you. Because they aren't flashy or clever, it takes you a while to realize that you have a treasure right under your nose. Once you see their qualities you come to love them deeply, with a quiet passion. To start with I didn't 'get' meditation on the breath. It was so simple that I couldn't believe there was much in it. But over the ensuing years I practised it quite a bit, alongside more complex meditations, and the more of it I did, the deeper it became, and the more I saw in it.

I belatedly realized that in the short time it took to learn the basics of the breathing meditation, I had been given a way of using my body and mind that has a host of benefits. We are all unique, and everyone will have their own experience, but having watched many hundreds of people practise this meditation over the years, I can say that anyone who practises it sincerely will experience some, if not all, of these benefits:

heightened awareness and enriched experience
The breath is your most fundamental experience of life, and bringing awareness to it can make you more alive. We are not very often present in our experience. We are deadened by a weight of habitual responses and our energy is caught up in obsessive

thinking and concerns. This simple but profound meditation helps you to come to life, to savour your presence in the world. You'll learn to be more conscious, more alive in your experience, to notice in more detail how you use your body and your mind. As a result you'll come to know yourself much better. This awareness also makes the world brighter; you'll notice more shades of colour, more subtleties in people's expressions. Your whole experience becomes richer.

greater freedom

This heightened awareness gives you more choice, and without choice you have no freedom. You have power over your life only to the extent that you are aware of what is going on. Much of who we are and how we live happens 'below our radar' in more or less unconscious physical, emotional, and mental habits – all kinds of things that we don't notice about our-selves, from little mannerisms to emotional tenden-cies – such as doing things we don't really want to do in order to please other people. Meditation gives you the awareness to see and feel what is going on, so that you can choose whether to carry on acting in the old ways or to find new, more creative ways of living. In fact, this heightened awareness itself tends to dis-solve old, fixed ways of being – like shedding a skin that is too tight.

more calm and less stress

Through this practice you'll learn to become more re-laxed, and to let physical tensions dissolve. Your mind's tendency to jump from one idea to the next like a computer-game character on amphetamines is replaced by a deepening stillness. In this stillness, all discursive thinking may even completely die away, leaving an expansive awareness that is deeply restorative.

better concentration and more happiness

In a world in which the sound-bites get ever shorter as people's attention spans diminish, this meditation teaches you how to give your full attention to one thing. This faculty can be developed so that, like a top athlete, you can tune out distractions and be totally 'in' what you are doing. If you think about it, you will recognize that concentration and happiness often go together. You are usually at your happiest when you are totally focused on one activity, such as listening to music or communicating deeply with someone. In those situations, as more and more of your energy becomes engaged, you feel very alive and fulfilled. Through this meditation you can take this capacity to new heights.[1] In fact, the Buddhist texts describe people practising this meditation sometimes experiencing states of intense bliss and rapture.

improved health

Over time, the meditation promotes deeper, smoother breathing, which has major health benefits.

---

1 This meditation is sometimes called the mindfulness of breathing. The suffix 'ful' originally meant 'having, or full of'. This suggests the meditation is about having awareness of your breathing, or, more poetically, letting the breath, your object of concentration, fill your mind.

(The volume of the breath has been shown to be a primary indicator of lifespan – the more air you take in, the longer you are likely to be around.)[2]

For those who like to have proof of these things, all this is increasingly being backed up by scientific research. Even a couple of months of meditation practice has been shown to provide a harvest of benefits. Recent research has shown that experienced Buddhist meditators are calmer and happier, less anxious and stressed than the average person. They have stronger immune responses and recover more quickly from influenza. They are more perceptive about the emotional states of those around them, picking up subtle cues from people's faces. (In some research in the United States, people from different walks of life were shown pictures of men and women in different emotional states and asked to guess how they were feeling. Not surprisingly, perhaps, secret service agents came out best, until the researchers tested some Buddhist meditators, who had even higher scores.)[3]

Good as all this is, from the Buddhist point of view, we still haven't mentioned the best reason for taking up this meditation. Buddhism is very radical. It believes it is possible to be very deeply happy and fulfilled, and to achieve that it is prepared to look the

2 *Science News*, vol.120, 1981, p.74, referenced on www.breathing.com
3 Lutz, A. *Proceedings of the National Academy of Science*, online early edition (www.pnas.org), Nov. 8, 2004. Daniel Goleman, 'Finding Happiness', *New York Times* (www.nytimes.com), February 4, 2003.

existential facts of life squarely in the eye. OK, so this meditation can help you recover quicker from flu: big deal. Perhaps it will even increase your lifespan, but still sooner or later you're going to grow old (if you get that far), get sick, and finally stop breathing altogether. It's that existential situation, those basic life issues, that Buddhism is really interested in addressing.

Nowadays, meditations on the breath are becoming commonplace. They are often taught in yoga classes, on stress management courses, and as part of some Western therapies. In those contexts you won't hear much talk about ageing and death. For many people that's fine. They don't think about these things, apart from at odd times when they are lying awake at three in the morning, or someone they know dies unexpectedly. And certainly you can read this book and learn the basics of Buddhist meditation without having to address those issues.

But some people are drawn to meditation for those very reasons. Yes, they want to be calmer and happier. But on a deeper level something in them wants real answers to some very straight questions: 'Who am I? What is life about? Why are we here?' 'What happens when we die?' Buddhist meditation gives you ways to approach those fundamental questions. Its methods help you to focus clearly on the raw material of your experience and find direct, intuitive answers to these issues. These answers based on direct experience go much deeper, and are far more satisfying, than any theories your everyday rational mind can come up with.

In order to get to those intuitive answers you need first to be able to make your mind sharp, calm, and clear. This is where all those earlier benefits come in. Most of this book will be concerned with achieving that clarity and serenity. On that basis, if you want to go deeper into Buddhist meditation you can do so. But in Buddhism, even when you first learn this meditation on the breath, that existential context is always there. Fundamentally, what makes something a Buddhist meditation isn't that it was passed down through some line of Buddhist teachers. What really makes it Buddhist is that it helps you to find answers to the most basic issues for you as a human being.

Buddhism uses many forms of meditation, but meditation on the breath is perhaps the most widespread and is found from Thailand to Tibet, and Tokyo to, nowadays, Toronto. The practice has been used since the time of the Buddha, so there is a deep experience and understanding of it within the tradition. It is very simple, so it is an excellent method for newcomers to meditation. But it is also very deep, so people who have been meditating for many years continue to practise it. It has a *number of advantages* that perhaps make it unique among meditations:

> It is *simple to learn*. You don't need to know any-thing about Buddhist philosophy, or believe anything particular. It is completely experience-based.

It is *always available*. The breath is portable. Even if you have only a couple of minutes available, you can tune in to it.

It is *suitable for all types of people*. Some forms of meditation are recommended for people of a particular character or aptitude, but this is one that anyone can practise and benefit from.[4]

As it has been used for so long in the Buddhist tradition (over 2,500 years), it is completely *tried and tested*. This also means that the ways in which the meditation can develop, and the experiences you are likely to have as you practise it over time, are very well charted.

Now, looking back over years of practice, I can see clearly the tremendous good that has come from what I learned on that cold winter's evening. Over the intervening years I have taught the meditation myself, and I know hundreds, if not thousands, of people who have practised it. I find it hard to think of anything else that can be imparted so quickly and yet have such a deep effect on someone's life. The only thing that comes to mind is something like learning the 'kiss of life', which is also connected with the breath. The kiss of life, of course, is literally life-saving, enabling the flow of the breathing to

---

4 The only proviso being that if you have a history of mental illness you should consult your physician and a qualified meditation teacher before taking it up. This applies to all forms of meditation.

continue. But unless our life is at risk, the main issue for us is how dead or alive we are in our life, whether our existence is something meaningful that we savour, or something dull that we wander through on autopilot. Meditation on the breath is life-enhancing, it brings you more fully alive, and awakens you to the richness and wonder of being human.

So I hope I have whetted your appetite, and that you will try out the methods and suggestions in this book. In most people's lives these days time is at a premium. Very often finding even fifteen or twenty minutes to do something new requires difficult negotiations – with family, friends, colleagues, and often with yourself. But this is time that will help you do everything else in a more relaxed and alive way – and time that you use for venturing deeper into what it means to be a human being, exploring the deep mystery of consciousness, is always time well spent.

how to use this book
People like to read in different ways. Some like to munch their way steadily from page one through to the final sentence, others prefer to graze here and there. You can take either approach and still gain from this book. What is crucial is that you try out the meditation. Like any practical skill or art, you have to do it in order to benefit from it. Also, if you experiment with the meditation, you will have some experience of your own to draw on as you read.

The main instructions for the meditation are contained in the first two chapters. You don't have to wait until you have worked through all the suggested meditation sessions there before you read Chapters 3 and 4. In fact, after you have tried out a bit of meditation, some of the hints and tips in Chapter 3 and the advice on how to start and end the meditation session in Chapter 4 may be very helpful. Chapter 5 looks at helpful and unhelpful attitudes to your practice, and will probably have the most impact once you have a few meditations under your belt. The last three chapters go deeper, with Chapter 6 looking at practical ways to develop things after you have had more experience, and the final two chapters giving you a sense of where meditation on the breath can take you.

While you can learn the basics of meditation from a book like this one, if you want to go deeply with it there is no substitute for finding a teacher. Someone more experienced can save you going down blind alleys, encourage and inspire you if you go through a dull patch, and set the meditation practice in a wider context of ways of understanding life and transforming your mind. Fortunately, there are many classes and courses in Buddhist meditation available these days. The best thing would be to read this book in conjunction with a meditation class. As I've mentioned, meditation on the breath is very widespread in the Buddhist tradition and elsewhere, so people inevitably have varying approaches. You may find that the meditation is taught slightly differently. If so, I suggest you practise the method that your teacher gives you, and use this book as background reading to give you helpful suggestions and inspiration.

1

trying out the practice

In essence, meditation is a way of exploring your experience, of diving into it and being alive to it. So the best method of learning it is direct, by trying it out. In this chapter we shall do just that, and start straight in to gain some experience of focusing on the breath. In later chapters I'll introduce you to a more structured form of the meditation and then suggest ways in which you can refine your practice.

This chapter gives you ideas for six introductory sessions of meditation. Although I have described them as introductory, feel free to go at your own pace. If you want, you can do several periods of meditation following the instructions for a particular session.

Although I have introduced them assuming no prior knowledge of the meditation, they may well be useful for those with some – or even a lot of – experience of this kind of practice. It is always useful to freshen up your approach by going back to square one. After I had been meditating for a few years I still used to enjoy sitting in on introductory classes. To be led through the basics of the practice brought them to life for me again, and I was often struck by details whose significance I hadn't recognized, even though I had heard them many times before. This open, fresh approach is highly valued in Buddhism.

before and after
In Chapter 4 we shall look in detail at ways in which you can prepare yourself for the meditation, and we shall also look more at bringing the meditation to an end. For now, prepare yourself by just sitting down comfortably. Find a position in which you are relaxed but alert, and gently close your eyes. Bring yourself into the present moment, and spend a few moments becoming aware of your body, feeling the sensations within it: its temperature, solidity, the energy associated with it. Then turn your attention to your breathing, making sure that you are breathing through your nose.[5] Then follow the suggestions for one of the six sessions below.

When you are ready to stop, just widen out your attention from your breath to take in your experience of your body once again, gently open your eyes and

---

5 If possible, you should breathe through your nose when practising any of the meditations described in this book. If you have a heavy cold, then your options are to breathe through your mouth, or meditate by bringing awareness to the breadth of your experience (see p.46).

take in your surroundings, and then get up in your own time, not rushing, but with a sense of spaciousness and calm as you prepare to move on to whatever you are doing next.

exploring the breath

session one
exploring your experience of the breath
Fundamentally, meditation isn't about techniques. So rather than giving you any techniques or methods, in this first session I'd like you to practise 'freestyle'. Begin by preparing yourself as described above. Once you have spent a little time being aware of your body, bring your attention to your breathing. Take time to explore the sensations of the breath in any way you like. Just tune in to the experience of breathing. Don't make this a very serious task. Keep a sense of lightness, even playfulness, as you find out how it feels to be breathing right now. Approach your breath like a child with a new toy, a dog with a new smell. See what you can find out about it. And if possible, enjoy it. After all, if the breath wasn't there you wouldn't be alive. Feel the life in your body as you take in air and give it back to the world around you.

Carry on exploring the breath in this way for as long as you like. But beware a superficial response after a few seconds of, 'Oh yes, in, out, there's the breath, that's it.' If that is your response, then note it, and sit a little longer to see any subtleties that come into awareness. If you go to an art gallery you will often see tourist parties walking around and hardly stopping. They recognize things and tick them off: 'Ah yes, the *Mona Lisa*; oh look, water lilies ...' but they have hardly experienced the paintings at all. Then you will occasionally see someone standing in front of a picture for minutes on end, looking and looking, noticing more and more details. It's almost as if they go right into the painting, they lose themselves in it, and in that way they experience something of the state of mind of the artist who created it. So give yourself time to go beyond your usual level of experience of your breathing, time for a new awareness of it to develop.

If your mind wanders off to other things, gently bring it back to the breath. When you have had enough, slowly bring yourself out of the meditation in the way that I suggested.

session two
following the breath into the lungs

Although meditation isn't about techniques, there are methods that can help to focus your mind on the breath. So once you have explored your breathing in a freestyle way, in this session you can try out a method called following the breath. Again, find a way of sitting in which you can be relaxed while remaining alert, close your eyes, bring yourself into the present moment, then bring your interest and attention to your breathing.

Once you have homed in on your experience of breathing, begin to follow each breath from beginning to end. Feel the sensation of the in-breath in your nostrils; let your awareness flow with it down into your lungs. Be the lungs as they expand and fill with air. Feel the point at which the in-breath is complete, fulfilled, and then sense the first signs that the out-breath is under way. Flow upwards with the air, from the lungs to the upper chest, to the throat, to the nostrils. Then hold your awareness at the nostrils until the next breath begins to flow inwards. Keep following the breath in this way for as long as you like, then end the session as before.

session three
following the breath to the abdomen
In this session you will be following the breath further into your abdomen. We know that the air only fills our lungs, but the process of breathing involves movement lower down in the body. The powerful action of your diaphragm causes movement in your belly. In experience, it can feel as if the breath is a wave that goes all the way down to your lower abdomen.

Prepare as usual, and then bring your attention to the breath. You may find it helpful to start by taking two or three deeper breaths before allowing the breathing to find its own rhythm. This stabilizes the mind a little before you begin. It also helps to underline for yourself your intention to bring all your awareness to bear on the breath.

Now follow the breath by feeling the wave of movement that it causes. Track the movements and sensations of each in-breath, from your nostrils all the way down to your abdomen. (For this session you might want to try placing your hands over your abdomen so that you can sense the movement more easily.) Then follow the out-breath back to the nostrils again.

Meditate in this way until you feel it is time to stop. Then come out from the meditation gradually.

When I teach breath meditation to newcomers there is always quite a spectrum of initial experiences. At one end are people who find they can hardly keep their minds on the breath at all. At the other, there are one or two who have experiences of deep peace and happiness. The majority find it interesting to explore the breath and notice that it has a calming effect, though their concentration comes and goes. These early experiences, however, don't give much of a guide to how meditation will affect you over time. If you did find concentration a struggle then you might want to start dipping into Chapter 3, which looks into reasons for that, and things you can do about it. And if you had a fantastic experience, then I'm very happy for you! But please don't insist to yourself that your next meditation should be the same. When you try to recreate the past you lose your openness to new experience, and that gets in the way of the meditation going deeper.

session four
letting go of the breath
The first three sessions started you off on a voyage of discovery, exploring your experience of breathing.

These next three continue that process and highlight particular qualities that really help you to meditate. This session focuses on relaxation and letting go.

Prepare yourself to meditate, then follow your breath to your abdomen as before. As you focus on your breathing, pay particular attention to letting go and relaxing. When you begin to meditate there is often a tendency to want to control your breath. This usually comes from judgements that you make about it. When you turn your awareness to it, you may find that your breath is fast, shallow, or uneven. You might not like it like that, or you might have an idea that it is supposed to be slow, deep, and steady. So you give it a nudge in that direction by controlling it. Certainly there are some yoga and ch'i kung exercises in which you do control the breath, but this meditation works in a different way. It is most effective when you let go, for the time being, of all judgements about your experience, all ideas of how you want it to be, and let it be how it is.

So throughout this session, make a practice of letting go of any effort to control the breath. Let the breath, and the wisdom of your body, guide you. Simply follow it with your awareness, wherever it leads. The breath has been around as long as you have; it's an adult. So don't be nannyish, trying to control it. Give it its freedom. Once you learn to do this you will find that your meditation will deepen and become much more relaxing.

session five
being the breath

One of the common words used to describe the unsatisfactoriness of twenty-first-century living is 'alienation'. We feel estranged from aspects of our experience, not at home in our lives. Meditation is a wonderful way to overcome this sense of separation from life. As you try to focus on the breath, you will certainly find that you are sometimes distanced from it. The breath feels like an object 'over there' (or perhaps 'down there' as you seem to watch it from up in your head somewhere), which you are experiencing from outside. One of the aims of meditation is to help you to be in your experience, to be in the flow of your life, the flow of your breath. This has very positive benefits in terms of releasing energy.

In this session you will be following the breath once again as it goes from your nostrils to your abdomen and back. However, this term, 'following the breath', may set you on the wrong track. You don't follow it like a flight controller tracking a plane on a radar monitor. The aim is to reduce the distance between yourself and the breath, to *be* the breath. Be the flow of air that cascades into your lungs. Be the movement of your rib cage. Be the diaphragm as it expands downwards with the in-breath and releases upwards with the out-breath. If you merge your awareness with your experience in this way, it will have a tremendous effect. We are too often passive spectators of life. Through this meditation you learn to become one with what is happening, to be in the flow of your life in an aware way.

Don't be concerned if you still felt a big gap between yourself and the breath during this session. The main thing at this stage is to get a sense of the direction in which you are trying to move in the meditation. The long-term aim is to be more in your experience. So you can begin to notice, in a meditation session or in your daily life, times when you are more engaged, more in your body, in your senses, and times when you aren't. If you keep taking a friendly interest in your experience, you will begin to feel the difference between those two states, and naturally learn how to move in the direction of more direct experience.

session six
keeping beginner's mind

In this session I suggest you continue to follow your breath down into your abdomen. As you do so, do your best to approach each breath in as fresh a way as you can. Because we have all been breathing since before we can remember, we very often take it for granted. In meditation we aim to experience everything with what Zen Buddhism calls 'beginner's mind'. When you are new to something, you don't know what to expect, so you are open to all kinds of possibilities and potentials. One of the aims of meditation is to help you peel away stale ideas and assumptions about life and to experience it directly, to find the freshness and vitality in it. After all, life is new every second. The breath is constantly changing and no two breaths are ever exactly the same. In this session the aim is to experience that for yourself.

It will help to do this if you lay aside all that you think you know about your breath and come at it from a new perspective. How do you know that you're breathing? What does it feel like? Explore your experience as if you were having it for the very first time.

Let yourself revel in your experience of the breath. After all, if you had just survived some life-threatening situation and were delighted to find yourself still alive and breathing, you would savour each lungful of air like a precious treasure.

conclusion

In these six sessions you've already come a long way. You've learned a method of meditation: following the breath. You've also had some experience of three of the most important principles of meditation on the breath:

> relaxing and letting go:
> not controlling the breath

> engaging directly with your experience:
> being the breath

> freshness and beginner's mind:
> seeing each breath as new

These three principles are important for any kind of meditation. In fact they're important for living happily and creatively. One of the main aims of meditation is to give you positive experiences that you can apply in everything you do. Working with the breath in these three ways holds important lessons, such as the value of living in a more relaxed way, of being alive to and in your senses and engaging directly with life, and keeping a fresh vision of things and being open to new possibilities and potentials, not taking life – or the people in it – for granted.

Of course, all this won't happen overnight. Meditation is a way of training your mind to respond in more creative ways – that is why we refer to it as a practice. Like any training, it takes time and gentle, steady effort. But if you keep meditating then after a while you will definitely begin to experience results. This is one of the great things about meditation: because you are working directly on your mind, the effects cannot be lost. In ordinary life you can sweat away at something and then lose out completely. For instance, you could put years of work into building up a business and then for reasons completely beyond your control – a stock-market slump, a new tax regime, increased competition – you could find yourself left with nothing to show for all that time and energy. I had a small experience of this recently. During the summer I trained for and ran a half-marathon and was very fit, but a few weeks later a bout of flu left me weak and tired, and most of the effects of all that effort vanished. However, the fruits of the work that you put into your own mind can't be lost or taken away from you. You always reap benefits sooner or later.

2

systematic practice: the four-stage method

In the previous chapter you learned to meditate on the breath in quite a simple way, just bringing your awareness to your breathing and following it in and out of your body. For some people this will be all the technique they need, but newcomers to this meditation usually find it helpful to have more of a structure. Using a structure takes away any uncertainty about what you should be doing; it also makes you aware of when your mind loses its clarity. You notice when you are no longer following the form of the meditation and this helps you to keep your focus on the breath. Best of all, a well-designed structure helps lead you step by step into deeper states of concentration.

In this chapter we're going to explore a four-stage approach to the breath. This is the method I was introduced to back in 1973 and I have taught it to many people. In the first two stages you use the method of counting the breath in different ways. This gives your mind, which is often restless when you start to meditate, a bit more to do, a task to engage with. In the last two stages you dispense with the counting and simply focus on the breath – first in a more general way and then very precisely.

To practise this method, set aside fifteen to twenty minutes during which you won't be disturbed. As the meditation has four stages, you'll aim to move on from one stage to the next every three to five minutes. You can either estimate this from your sense of time passing or you can put a watch or clock in front of you and glance at it occasionally. Don't worry about trying to make the stages exactly equal; that isn't important.

Begin as usual by sitting comfortably, finding a posture that is relaxed and alert. Now bring your attention to your breathing, remembering to let the breath decide how it wants to be. You aren't trying to change or control it; just let it flow naturally. Develop a sense of interest in what the breath is like, experiencing it as if for the first time. As you become interested in your breathing you will find that the sense of separation between you and the breath becomes less. Do your best to experience it directly, to *be* the breath, not a distant observer of it.

Once your mind has 'found' the breath and started to engage with it, you can begin the first stage of the meditation itself.

stage one
counting after the out-breath

At the end of the next out-breath silently count 'one' to yourself. Then feel the next in- and out-breath, and at the end of that silently count 'two'. Continue silently counting after each out-breath in this way, so after the next out-breath you inwardly say 'three' – or if you prefer you can visualize the numbers in your mind. Carry on doing this until you reach ten, and then begin the process again, so that after the eleventh out-breath you count 'one'.

(If you find the description in the last paragraph a bit laboured, it's because I know from experience that sometimes the instructions can be taken in ways that I hadn't intended. I've known people hold their breath for the count of 'one' for the first breath, 'two' for the second, etc. I've also known people who counted 'one' after the first breath, then 'one, two' after the second until by the tenth breath they were counting from one to ten. If when teaching I use the phrase, 'once you reach ten you go back to one' there will always be some people who count up to ten and then count backwards to one. All these misunderstandings were my fault, as I hadn't spelled things out clearly enough.)

Continue counting after the out-breath until you decide it is time to move on to the second stage.

stage two
counting before the in-breath

In the second stage, you continue using counting to help you to stay with the breath, but there is a subtle change in the point at which you insert the number. In this stage you count just as you sense the first beginnings of the in-breath, so this time you silently count 'one', then breathe in and out, then 'two' before the next in-breath, and continue in this way up to ten. Then start again from one.

Some people respond to this by saying, 'But you're counting in the same place as in the first stage. What's the difference?' The answer is that in the first stage you are looking backwards; the count marks the end of the previous breath. Here you are looking forwards, anticipating what is about to happen. Psychologically, these two experiences feel very different. Anticipation requires a greater degree of awareness. (Think of the difference between the awareness needed to notice that someone has just bumped into you, and having the awareness to see that you are on a collision course.) So in practice this second stage feels different from the first, and usually leads you into a sharper, more awake experience of the breath. During this stage, your awareness of the first signs of another breath starting on its way can become finer and finer.

Counting after the out-breath tends to make you pay most attention to the exhalation, whereas counting before the in-breath tends to heighten your awareness of the inhalation. Focusing on the exhalation promotes relaxation, while emphasizing the inhalation energizes the body. So through these two stages you first practise letting go and then you gather in energy. As you become familiar with using the counting through repeated practice, see if you can experience these processes for yourself. How do the two stages differ in your experience?

After you have spent some time using counting to anticipate the next breath, it is time to move on to the third stage.

points about the counting to be aware of
The counting is not your main focus of attention. Your aim in these two stages is to deepen your interest in the breath. What is it like today? How does it feel? How shallow or deep is it? Where do you feel it most strongly? Counting just gives your mind a way of marking each breath. It is another way to engage with it. Counting also acts as an early warning system, helping you to notice when you have drifted away from the breath. You may no longer know what number you have reached or you may find you have counted on past ten. These are indicators that you have lost your engagement with the breath. When this happens, don't give yourself a hard time. Meditation is a skill that we learn. If we could do it perfectly we wouldn't need to practise it. Feeling irritated or disappointed with yourself for losing track of the breath is just another distraction to add to your original one. Don't make a drama out of it; we all lose count. Even experienced meditators have days when they lose the plot with the counting and have to go

back to square one, so when it happens to you, just calmly come back to an awareness of your body, then feel your way back to what is happening with the breath. When you have engaged with it again, restart the count with 'one' and continue as before.

stage three
experiencing the whole breathing process
In this stage you drop the counting. The counting was a support, giving your mind another reason to pay attention to the breath. But as your interest in the breath deepens, the counting is no longer necessary. In fact it may even start to feel like a distraction. If your mind is becoming absorbed in the actual experience of breathing, then it may be counter-productive to have to step out, even momentarily, from the flow of the breath in order to pay attention to the next number.

Having let go of the count, you simply follow the breath. You experience the progress of each breath from the nostrils down to the lungs and back. You can also become aware of the movement of the abdomen and of anything else that contributes to your sense that you are breathing. In this way you experience the whole breathing process. You give yourself up to the experience of the breath, feeling all the various sensations that go to make it up and relaxing into them. It is a little like going to a beach, wading into the sea, and then just letting yourself float, enjoying the rise and fall of the waves. You're not swimming, not trying to go anywhere, you're just allowing the waves to cradle you.

In the same way, you just let the breath be itself, giving yourself up in an aware way to the constantly changing sensations as each breath flows in and then ebbs away. If you're very relaxed and have let go of the breath, it can feel as if the breathing is just happening by itself, that rather than breathing you are being breathed.

When you have spent a few minutes experiencing the whole of the breath, it is time to move on to the final stage.

stage four
focusing on one point
You have been building up concentration by generating awareness of your whole breathing process. In this last stage you turn all that accumulated mental power on to one point, like kindling a fire by focusing the sun's rays through a magnifying glass. You home in on the point where you first feel the subtle sensation of the air coming into the body.

To do this you begin by taking your awareness to the area around your upper lip and the entrance to your nostrils. How do you know from your experience in this area that you are breathing? You will feel subtle sensations, maybe a slight tickling or brushing of the air and a sensation of coolness as the incoming breath flows over your skin. These first signs of the air coming in may be on your upper lip or perhaps inside your nostrils. Wherever you feel these sensations, take a real interest in them; put all your awareness and attention there.

In the previous stage, your attention flowed in and out like the tide as you followed the breath. In this stage you don't follow the breath into your body; instead, you keep your focus anchored at one spot. You feel the sensations as the air comes past that point on its way in and out. Imagine yourself to be a gatekeeper or janitor who knows everyone's business, watching intently to see who passes in and out of the property. You are aware of every stage of the traffic of the air in and out of your body and you never desert your post.

This last stage leads your mind into deeper levels of concentration. This is because there is a dynamic interplay between your awareness and your breathing. In order to experience the delicate sensations of the air, you need to pay close attention, and that greater attentiveness changes your breathing pattern. The breath will most likely become more refined, which means that the sensations around your nostrils become subtler, which in turn causes you to focus more strongly in order to stay with them. This creates a 'virtuous circle' in which increased concentration leads to more exquisitely delicate sensations which require your concentration to be even better attuned.

In this way, when the practice goes well, breath and awareness dance together, leading each other into more refined realms of experience. You may even arrive at a point at which the sensations become too subtle to find. At that point the natural tendency is to 'rev up' the breath, making it stronger so that you can feel it again. But this may disturb the harmony of the concentrated state that you have built up, so if you can't find the breath it is best to wait patiently, staying aware of the point where you last experienced it.

When you have spent a few minutes gently focusing attention on the sensations where you feel the air entering and leaving your body, slowly disengage your attention from them. Widen out your awareness until you feel your whole body, and then bring the meditation to a close.

To summarize, these are the four stages.

1. counting after each out-breath

2. counting before each in-breath

3. dropping the counting and experiencing your whole breathing process

4. focusing on the point where you first experience the breath

As well as giving your mind a framework to practise within, the four stages take it on a journey of increasing refinement in which it engages more and more deeply with the experience of breathing.

the magician's apprentice
Let's look at an analogy that can make the development of the meditation through the four stages clearer. Imagine a magician who takes on a young

man as an apprentice. To start with the youth is very dull and unaware and doesn't even register the unusual happenings around the magician. But the wise magician feels that, despite appearances, this young man has hidden potential, so in order to bring it out he gives him a task. He sits his apprentice on a wall by a path and tells him that he owns a large number of horses. The magician will drive them down the path and the apprentice's task will be to count them, one by one.

The young man sits dozily on his wall in the sunshine. After a while he hears the sound of the magician chanting a spell, and some animals come by, their manes, flanks, and tails bright in the sunlight. He isn't very interested in horses and his mind keeps drifting off. But he has a job to do, so he pays enough attention to keep count, though often only just in time, counting as the animals have gone by and are disappearing into the distance.

The apprentice soon realizes that by counting like that he might miss a fast-moving horse, as it could disappear out of sight before he has registered it. So he shakes himself more awake and begins watching the horses as they come towards him, counting them as they come into view.

As he pays a bit more attention to them in this way, he becomes dimly aware, still in a rather dozy state, that there is something very odd about these horses. Forgetting all about the counting, he starts to scan each animal from head to tail, looking at each one intently in order to work out what is unusual about it.

When he does this it dawns on him at once. If he had not been half asleep, functioning on automatic and taking his experience for granted, he would have seen it straight away. These aren't horses at all. They're unicorns! Each one has a spiral horn on its forehead. Now he forgets all about the manes, bodies, hooves, and tails. With each creature that passes his whole attention is focused on that wondrous horn. As time goes on, and he becomes more and more engrossed in the horns, he finds himself following their spiral shape until his attention is poised on the very point of the horn itself. In this way, the apprentice moves from a dull state to an aware one, and finally into a magical realm in which his attention is riveted on what he is experiencing.

Our experience of this meditation may not be as exciting as the four stages of the apprentice's experience, but if we keep practising we shall come to see that the breath has a magic of its own.

setting up a regular practice

What you have learned in these first two chapters is all you really need to establish a regular meditation practice – if you wish to do so. So if you do want to take things further and embark on the ongoing adventure of meditation, here are answers to some practical questions that many people ask.

how long should I meditate for?

I suggest that you start with sessions of about fifteen to twenty minutes. You could use the four-stage method and spend three to five minutes on each stage. If you have more time, you can gradually lengthen your sessions as your body and mind grow more accustomed to meditation. One way to do this without getting stiff and uncomfortable physically is to do a period of meditation then go for a short walk (not too brisk), keeping a thread of awareness of your breathing, then come back and do another period of sitting meditation.

As I mentioned earlier, you can time the meditation with a watch or clock in front of you, and occasionally check how the time is going. After you have been meditating for a few months you will probably find that you can set an 'internal timer' that enables you to judge pretty accurately how much time has passed in meditation.

what is the best time of day?

This is largely a matter of temperament and metabolism. Some people take an hour or so to surface in the mornings, and find meditation at that time a struggle. Others are up with the lark (or the sound of the first bus), but run out of steam by mid-evening. If you are a very definite morning or evening person then you should take that into account. But many people fall somewhere between those two extremes. If so, the best time to meditate is probably first thing in the morning. This has the advantage that your mind will not be processing the events of the day. Morning meditation will also energize you and sharpen you up for the day ahead. But if you don't have the time to meditate early in the day, never mind. Whenever you do it, meditation will have a beneficial effect.

where should I practise?
At home, it's usually best to meditate in the same place each time. Try to find somewhere that is quiet and undisturbed. If you can do it, it is helpful to dedicate a space in your home to meditation, and make it as conducive for you to meditate as possible. You might want to put some flowers or other natural things there, or pictures of scenes or people that have a calming or inspiring effect on you. Taking these things in as you sit down helps to put you in a relaxed and meditative mood. Meditating outdoors can also be a special experience.

how often should I practise?
It is up to you. But, like anything else, if you want to improve and gain the maximum benefit, then regular practice is essential. As with learning a language or going to the gym, little and often is far more effective than doing nothing for a while and then rushing to try to make up for lost time.

For best results, you can't beat a daily practice. However short, daily meditation gives you a sense of continuity and allows the positive effects to build up. If you can set up a daily routine, then after a few months you'll find that meditation becomes natural. Once you get to that point, missing a day's practice feels like a real loss.

3

now that you've had some experience...

The last two chapters gave you all the practical groundwork you need in order to start meditating on the breath. I hope that by now you've given it a go. If not, I urge you to just sit where you are, if appropriate, close your eyes, and try it out. The topics we shall be looking at now will make much more sense if you have had some experience of your own.

In this chapter I've distilled a lot of practical experience that has come out of my practice, and from discussing this meditation with Buddhist teachers, friends, and people I have taught over the years. The sections all cover issues that newcomers (and more experienced – sometimes even very experienced – meditators) come face to face with time and time again, in relation to meditation in general and this meditation in particular. You may find that some of what I say definitely applies to you while other points don't resonate with your experience. I suggest you

take on board what you find helpful and file the rest
away for possible future use.

the mind's tendency to go its own way

The first thing to understand is that it's entirely natural for your mind to wander away from the breath
during the meditation. Nobody, except perhaps very
experienced meditators living blissfully undisturbed
in some remote retreat, can go through this practice
day after day without distraction. When I first
learned this meditation I had a few sessions where
everything was new and fresh and I became very concentrated. But then, as meditation became more
everyday and less special, I soon found that I often
struggled to find the breath for more than a few
seconds at a time. I felt like a shipwreck survivor
clinging to a spar – the breath – while great waves of
thought crashed over me. Their tremendous pull
frequently dragged me under. I would surface seconds or minutes later and then swim back to the distant spar, get a loose grip on it, and then be washed
away by yet more feelings and ideas.

This is where most of us start. In fact I have sometimes
joked to people doing publicity for meditation
courses that, if they were completely honest, their
advertisements would read, 'Learn to meditate and
discover what a mess your mind is.' The realization
that most of the time it is hard work to count ten
breaths (or even three on some days) comes as a shock
to most people. When it happened to me, I felt as if
the meditation was making my mind worse or as if I
went a bit haywire when I sat down to meditate. But

that wasn't the case. Through asking me to focus on one object, the breath, the meditation made me vividly aware of the unlikely parade of good ideas, bad ideas, plans, hopes, fears, sorrows, joys, memories, songs, daydreams, kind feelings, apparently random images, bits of unfinished conversations, etc., that passed through my mind all the time. But once I had discovered that my mind was like that, what was I going to do about it?

I remember a few years ago I was doing an intensive meditation retreat, by myself, in a wooden hut in the Spanish mountains. At one point I noticed that some giant ants had appeared and were climbing busily around the place. Every day there were more, until eventually I seemed to be hosting their national convention. At this rather late point I decided to track down what it was that made my hut so attractive to them. Eventually, I opened a cupboard drawer that was almost full of giant ants. I discovered some chocolate a friend had given me before the retreat. I had eaten a small piece and then put it away without thinking. The ants had found it and opened a chocolate mine. They had brought in thousands of workers, who were driven to work harder by chocoholic ant lieutenants. I disposed of the chocolate and within hours my visitors had vanished.

Exploring your mind in meditation is the equivalent of my becoming aware of the ants and looking round to see what had attracted them. When I opened that drawer there were far more ants than I had realized. But opening the drawer didn't produce them out of nothing. They were there all the time; I just hadn't noticed them.

At the point when you recognize that your mind is often out of your control, you have a choice similar to the one I had on finding the ants' chocolate mine. You can back off and give up meditating, which would be like quietly closing the drawer and deciding to live with the ants. Or you can get the whole thing out in the open, explore what is going on, and take steps to address the issue by keeping up a regular practice of exploring your mind through meditation.

If you do keep patiently meditating, then as time goes by you will find that the torrent of thoughts and feelings does start to slow. The great Indian yogi Tilopa said that at first the mind is like a turbulent mountain stream, but after some practice it becomes more like the gently-flowing Ganges.[6] And there will even be times when that flow ceases altogether, the chatter of your mind falls silent, and you become deeply immersed in the simple, rich, and fulfilling experience of the breath.

So if your mind surprised you by its busyness, don't let that put you off. For now, just take it as a valuable piece of information about yourself that the meditation has given you. As you read further, you will find suggestions for ways to improve this state of affairs.

---

6 See Tilopa's teaching to Naropa in, e.g., Thrangu Rinpoche, *The Ganges Mahāmudra*, Zhyisil Chokyi Publications, 2003.

enjoyment, interest, and a sense of purpose
In the previous section we looked at our tendency to
become sidetracked, to busy ourselves in meditation
with all kinds of things (some days it can feel like anything!) rather than our breathing. It is important to
explore this and to try to understand it. When your
mind has wandered away from the breath, what has
happened? If you look, you'll see that it usually
moves on to new pastures for the same reasons that
you switch television channels or give up on one
friendship and move on to another one: you aren't
enjoying it, you've lost interest, and/or you've lost
touch with why you were doing it in the first place.
Meditation may be different from your everyday
activities but the same kinds of emotional factors are
at play.

If that is why we lose our concentration, then the
solution to the problem must be to find enjoyment in
the breath, to develop our interest in it, and to keep in
touch with our reasons for doing it. These are three
key factors in meditation and, if we keep remembering them, the whole thing will flow much more easily.

enjoyment
When you are enjoying something, you naturally
want to keep your attention on it. When watching a
hot-air balloon rising into a clear summer sky or meeting your best friend after a long absence, you tend to
be effortlessly concentrated – so much so that you
don't think in terms of concentration at all. So one of
the secrets of successful meditation is to look for
sources of enjoyment within the practice. (Great, isn't

41

it? Here's something you can enjoy as much as you like, it's completely free, and it's good for you.) You can enjoy sitting quietly, having given this time to yourself. You can enjoy the flow of the breath, the silk thread of the air moving in and out. You can enjoy the sense of energy in your body as it is charged with oxygen.

This enjoyment needs to be natural, not forced. Cranking up a feeling of happiness or demanding of yourself that you have some Big Feeling just doesn't work. Keep it simple. Be patient. Just look around in your current experience for some seeds, some sources of enjoyment connected with the breath. When you find them, pay attention to them, let them grow.

Incidentally, what I have just said is not only true in the case of enjoyment, it also holds good for any other aspect of meditation that you are trying to develop. If you want to develop more calmness, say, then look around in your present experience and see if you can find something that feels as if it could become a feeling of tranquillity. Pay attention to it, feel its texture, enjoy it on its own level. Bringing on these shoots of helpful feeling is much more effective than trying to conjure up strong feelings out of thin air.

interest
As human beings we can derive enjoyment from simple pleasures – such as looking at a rainbow or feeling the calm flow of the air in our nostrils – but we also gain great satisfaction from learning and discovering. So it is very important to engage your interest and

curiosity in the meditation. The practice can become very absorbing if you think of it as exploring your experience. Meditation gives you a kind of close-up, intimate picture of yourself and there is always more to learn, all sorts of subtle areas that you can investigate. For instance, you can focus on different facets of the breath, noticing whether it is deep or shallow, coarse or fine, silent or noisy, easy or laboured, quick or slow. Or you can look for answers to questions like these: do you notice a difference in temperature between the in-breath and the out-breath? How is your breathing pattern affected by different thoughts and emotions? Is there always a gap between the in-breath and the out-breath? What causes it to grow longer, shorter, or disappear?

Looking into questions like these can teach you a great deal about your breathing but, because the breath interacts with the totality of your experience, you can also learn about your energy, your feelings, your thoughts, your intuition, in fact every aspect of yourself. If you approach each meditation as a chance to discover more about yourself, then the practice becomes a real adventure.

sense of purpose

Perhaps this is the golden key. After all, you can even do things that you don't enjoy and aren't interested in if you have a strong enough sense of purpose. For instance, you might hate parties but still go to one in order to give pleasure to a good friend. I'm mentioning this not so that you forget about enjoyment and interest, but in order to point out that a deep sense of purpose is an even more decisive factor for concentrated meditation. So if your mind keeps on going AWOL from the breath, it is a good bet that you have lost touch with your reasons for meditating. This is so important that it forms a vital part of the preparations for meditation that we'll look at in the next chapter.

As we'll see more and more, meditation is an art, a collection of skills that you bring to bear to produce something delightful and harmonious. What you create isn't a sculpture or a poem, it's an inner art work, a state of mind in which you are functioning at your best, with all your energy and awareness flowing in a unified stream. Some of the most crucial skills in this art are the finding of enjoyment, development of interest, and getting in touch with a strong sense of purpose. When all these are well developed and working together, meditation feels like the most natural thing in the world.

the breath is a means to an end

When I first began meditating on my breathing, I had a very narrow, literal-minded view of what I was supposed to be doing. I just aimed to focus on the breath and stay with it, ignoring anything else in my mind as a distraction. It was rather as though my mind was a wild horse I was riding, which was constantly trying to throw me off, and the breath was like its mane which I was hanging onto for dear life. It took a while for it to dawn on me that the real aim of the practice isn't to keep your mind on the breath. Your real purpose is to change your mind – to develop serenity, concentration, and other fulfilling ways to be. Paying attention to your breathing is just a means of helping you to develop those mental qualities.

So there are no gold stars to be won for clutching onto the breath in a grim, dogged fashion. I've known people who learned to stay with the breath in ways that were either dull and mechanical or very forced. (We shall look at some of these attitudes in Chapter 5.) They may have been able to count their breaths but they weren't on the right track with meditation. Your aim is to build alive, alert, and emotionally engaged mental states, using the breath as a tool to help you do that. In pursuit of that goal, you need to be flexible. At times the best way to fulfil your aims may be to stop trying to follow your breath.

Imagine you're trying to hold an important telephone conversation when, on the street below your open window, someone starts up a pneumatic drill. One possibility is that you squeeze the telephone receiver closer to your ear, close your other ear with your forefinger, and shout. That is the equivalent of holding on to the breath at all costs. Another possibility is that you interrupt the call to get up and close the window. That's clearly the more intelligent option. So in meditation you need to be prepared to let go of the breath when necessary. It's good to attend to other aspects of your experience if that helps you to deepen the calm and clarity of your mind.

For instance, suppose you are following the breath and finding it hard work. You try putting a little more energy into concentrating but that doesn't do the trick. At this point it could be wise to leave the breath temporarily in order to get a feeling for what is going on. What is happening in your experience that is making it hard to concentrate? As you explore your experience, suppose you find your meditation posture isn't right. Perhaps you are holding a lot of tension in your neck and shoulders. So then you deliberately take some time to relax your body until you are ready to come back to the breathing.

breadth and focus

This model of using the breath as a means, and being prepared to let go of it where necessary, is much better than a literal-minded 'just stay with the breath at all costs' approach. But, in order to judge when to stay with the breath and when to widen your interest, there is an important distinction to be made. There are essentially two kinds of concentrated states. One is a thin, narrow concentration, achieved usually by will-power, by holding the rest of your experience at bay. Meditations of this type can be enjoyable up to a point, but they are not very stable. It is as if you have taken a small bit of yourself and developed it in isolation, so that a representation of your mental state looks like a piece of chewing gum from which you have pulled out one long thin strip. The other form of concentration is a more natural one in which, rather than shutting out aspects of your experience, they all flow easily together to support your focus. This would look more like a pyramid, which has a solid base, and where the stone at the apex is supported by the rest of the structure.

In meditation we're aiming for that natural concentration in which awareness of the breath is supported by the rest of our experience. Focus on the breath always happens within the wider context of your total experience – your awareness of your surroundings, your physical posture, your feelings, what you are telling yourself, and so on. Rather than ignoring all that, it is good to allow your concentration on the breath to happen on the basis of it.

This means that effective meditation involves two factors.

> *breadth:* your overall awareness of what is happening with yourself, which provides the context for your concentration

> *focus:* homing in on your object of concentration, which here is your breath

How do you know when to broaden your awareness to take in more of your overall experience and when to focus more on your breathing?

As meditation is an art, you can to some extent only learn this from experience, by trial and error. But generally it is good to start by feeling the breadth of your experience. Rather than diving straight into focusing on the breath, it is helpful to come to it gradually. First of all, take in your total situation: the place where you're sitting, your meditation posture and how your body feels, your thoughts and feelings, your level of interest in the meditation. Then make adjustments to these as necessary, so that you are giving yourself the best context in which to focus. (In the next chapter we shall look in detail at a way of preparing to meditate that takes these factors into account.) When you've settled yourself in this way you will be in a much better position to give your full attention to the breath.

Once you have focused on your breathing, one approach is gently to broaden your awareness whenever you feel that by improving the context for your concentration you could draw more energy into the meditation. For example, if you find your focus on the breath is weak, you might widen your attention and realize that you have lost touch with your sense of purpose, your reason for meditating. Then you could look for something that inspires you to want to meditate, such as a sense of what you can gain from it, or a memory of a previous practice that went well and how that felt, which will give you more energy with which to focus on the breath again.

If you find you are repeatedly distracted, it is often helpful to broaden your awareness. Sometimes there is something specific that is drawing you away from the breath; maybe you're worried about something and can't put it down. In that case it is usually best to turn towards the disturbing thought or feeling: give it some attention, make it your concentration object for a little while. What is the quality of the feeling associated with it? What would satisfy it? You may not be with the breathing but, by doing this, you are moving in the direction of your overall meditation aims. True meditation is a state in which all the aspects of your-self flow harmoniously together. That can only come about from getting to know yourself more deeply and taking a kindly interest in your experience.

Sometimes you'll find that, although you are unable to concentrate, when you broaden your awareness there is nothing specific or obvious that needs atten-tion. In that case it is usually best to come back to a sense of your surroundings, particularly to your felt sense of your body, and rekindle your interest before you return to the breath.

If concentration is difficult, you can also experiment with keeping quite a breadth of awareness through-out the meditation – keeping a sense of your body, surroundings, feelings, and thoughts – and within that just put some attention on the breath, maybe twenty-five per cent. This lighter way of focusing is particularly good for people who tend to tense up and try too hard.

Although there is a great deal more that could be said about breadth and focus, once you understand the basic principle you can develop an intuition for how to put them into practice as your experience of medi-tation grows.

stepping back to guide the meditation
In the last section we saw that part of the art of medi-tation is learning about the interplay between breadth and focus. Generally I suggested that the most important times to develop a broad awareness

of your experience were at the beginning of a session and when you are finding there isn't much energy behind your concentration. But even if your mind is happily focused on the breath there is usually a way of going deeper, and you may only see this if you step back briefly and take stock. It is like an artist standing back from a canvas to take in the effect of recent work on it, or a marathon runner glancing at a watch to assess the pace and how far there is left to go.

So even during a meditation in which you are feeling engaged and interested, it's a good idea to take a few seconds out from the breath occasionally. One good time to do this is at the end of a stage before you embark on the next one. Step back and check how things are going. Take note of your posture: is it still alert and relaxed, or do you need to adjust it? Ask yourself about your level of engagement: are you keen to carry on with the practice, or have you let yourself become discouraged? How is your internal state now? In particular, how is your energy? If you are a little dull or drowsy then you need to take action to increase the energy you are putting into the practice. If you are a bit restless you need to calm and settle yourself. (We'll look at how to work with energy later in this chapter.)

With practice, taking stock of the meditation can be done very quickly. It's a kind of course correction: checking that you are on track in the practice, and making any necessary changes.

Although it's usually helpful to step back in this way from time to time, don't follow this advice slavishly; use your developing skill and judgement. If you do find yourself becoming naturally and deeply concentrated on the breathing then just go with that – don't feel you have to pull back and take stock, or develop more breadth, if that will just break up your party. Sometimes it is best to keep it very simple – just let the breath carry you along, and enjoy the ride.

making a balanced effort

The kind of effort you make in meditation is crucial for the whole process. Part of the art of meditation lies in gauging how much energy to put into it. This is a skill you acquire only by taking a friendly interest in your experience. If you treat yourself heavy-handedly you will make a crude effort to force things and end up frustrated and disappointed.

So with that friendly interest, one of the things you are checking for is to see that you are making an appropriate amount of effort. If you don't engage enough energy, your mind will go its own sweet way, moving from one distraction to the next like a goat munching its way across a hillside. You may also find that you become dull and sleepy. If you try too hard and apply too much energy, you will simply stir up your mind so that it buzzes around like a trapped bumble bee. In addition, you may well become restless and tense.

Somewhere between these two extremes there is a point of balance. You can learn to recognize when you have found the appropriate amount of energy because you feel light and aware, but also calm and relaxed. But finding it requires you to develop a subtle awareness of what is going on in your body and mind.

One way to learn balanced effort is by deliberately finding the extremes. So in meditation you could try spending a little time making an all-out effort to stay with the breath. Watch it like a hawk. Crank up your efforts until you feel you have definitely started to strain. (Don't completely overdo it.) Then relax back more and more. Keep relaxing and reducing your effort until you are sure you have become too laid back to stay with the breath. Having found these extremes, move between them, slowly reducing the amount of relaxation and the amount of effort, until you are trying to catch subtler and subtler movements to one side or other of the point of balance. Eventually you should find a state that combines relaxation and alert awareness. This is a useful exercise to do from time to time in order to develop a definite feeling for balanced effort. There is a whole art to finding the balance, as every time you sit to meditate the energy configuration of your body and mind are different.

Most Westerners err on the side of too much effort and need to focus more on relaxing and letting go. This is often because we don't have much real confidence in ourselves, so we make up for our lack of trust in the process of meditation by trying too hard. If you find you are habitually like this, it is good to spend time relaxing your body before you begin focusing on the breath (see the section on the body scan in the next chapter). However, I also know people who are wary of making a strong effort and never really bring all their energy to bear on anything. So it really is a question of experimenting and taking an intelligent interest in what is going on in order to discover your individual patterns and tendencies.

In general, you will probably need to invest more effort and energy at the beginning of the practice. It is like flying a large aircraft: a lot of fuel is used in revving the engines, trundling down the runway, and getting airborne. Once you're up, you throttle back and begin to cruise. In meditation you often need to make a good deal of effort to bring the mind onto the breath. Once it is settled on the breathing, you usually need less energy to maintain that concentration. In fact, if you keep making the same degree of effort you're likely to generate unnecessary tension and prevent yourself from going deeper.

A good demonstration of how people often try too hard is the 'final bell' syndrome. In group meditations the beginning, end, and different stages of the meditation are often marked by a gong or bell. It is quite common for someone to feel they are not getting anywhere in the meditation until the final bell goes. At that point, they're free to leave. So they relax … and hey presto, all of a sudden they fall into a much deeper state of meditation. It was their forceful effort that had been creating subtle resistance and holding them back.

working with energy

I talked earlier about the 'waves of thought' that washed over me much of the time during my early years of meditation and carried me away from concentrating on the breath. All meditators need to learn how to work with these difficulties. These obstacles to the meditation are of two main kinds. There are those where your mind's energy is going off in some other direction, such as when:

you are feeling angry or annoyed: you might be replaying a remark that someone at work made to you and feeling cross at the injustice of it, or you could be feeling irritated with your partner for leaving you to do the washing up.

your mind gets involved in attractive daydreams or imaginings: you could find yourself in imagination already on the holiday beach that you have booked to go to in the summer, or perhaps being invited out by your favourite actor or singer. The possibilities are endless, as we human beings have a great capacity to use our minds as a kind of built-in home entertainment system.

you feel restless physically or anxious mentally: your body may feel antsy or it may be hard to sit still – like a dog longing to be taken out and let off its leash; or you may be worried about money, your child's health, or being late for work if you get concentrated and meditate for too long.

Buddhist meditation manuals give specific advice for working with all these obstacles, but they are outside the scope of this short book.[7] For now, it is enough to recognize that all of them will respond to calming the mind.

On the other hand, far from feeling as if your energy is carrying you away from the meditation, there are times when you feel *heavy, tired, listless, or sluggish*. For instance, if you try to meditate just after some heavy physical work, you may feel in a kind of dull twilight zone, somewhere between waking and sleeping, mentally, and like a sack of potatoes physically. Obviously this is the opposite of the states in the previous paragraphs. It doesn't feel like a wave carrying you off, but more like an undertow pulling you down beneath the surface into unconsciousness. You may even find yourself almost dropping off to sleep and then waking abruptly – so you look a bit like one of those nodding dog ornaments. The antidote obviously isn't to calm the mind further (you'd probably end up on the floor) but to energize it.

So how do you work to calm or energize yourself in meditation?

---

7 For a good discussion of how to work with these hindrances see Kamalashila, *Meditation: The Buddhist Way of Tranquillity and Insight*, Windhorse Publications, 1999.

calming

We've seen that calming is for those times in meditation when you are busy planning your to-do list,
rehearsing a defence against your boss at work, or
daydreaming about the wonderful meditation you'll
have next week. The problem is that you are too much
in your head and probably in the past or future and
not enough in your body, in the here and now. Most
of the ways of working to change this involve bringing energy down lower in your body. For instance,
you can anchor your attention in your belly, just feeling the movement down there. You can also slow the
breathing a little, or take a few deeper breaths into
your abdomen. (It's OK to guide the breath in this
way for a short time in order to improve your meditation before letting it find its own natural rhythm
again.) Or you can focus particular attention on the
out-breath, with a sense of letting go and relaxing.
Another way to work is to imagine all the tension and
excess energy flowing down through your body deep
into the ground.

energizing

Energizing methods are for times when your sitting
posture has slumped, your mind has the consistency
of thick porridge, or when your eyelids weigh several
pounds each. Calming involves going lower or slower
and emphasizing the out-breath; energizing means
going higher or faster and focusing on the in-breath.
So when you feel dull and tired, it can help if you
concentrate on the breath high up in the body, perhaps taking a few deep breaths into your upper chest
or briefly breathing more lightly and quickly. Pay

particular attention to the in-breath and the sense of your body expanding and taking in energy as you do so. Light is also very energizing. If you are tired you can imagine yourself inhaling light with each breath. If you are meditating with your eyes closed you can open them so that you receive more stimulation. If you are drowsy, it can help if you turn up the lights or focus your attention on a candle for a while.

There is one other state that will impact on your meditation from time to time, and that is *doubt and uncertainty*. This may be uncertainty about whether to continue a particular meditation session, it may be unclarity about how to work in the meditation to achieve the best results, or it may be doubt about whether meditation works. Whatever form it takes, doubt has an undermining effect on your practice because it prevents you from making a wholehearted effort. It is easy to fall into a negative spiral: feeling unsure about whether the practice will work so not putting much energy into it, which means you won't get much result from it.

So whenever you notice that doubt has been nibbling away at your motivation, take steps to address it. In your current session, this may involve recommitting yourself – perhaps thinking, 'I'll do my best for five more minutes and then stop.' More generally, you may need to reflect and remind yourself of the benefits of meditation or read something that re-inspires you to practise. Sometimes there are deeper issues involved – genuine questions – and you should not push those away. A good way to work with them is to spend a few minutes concentrating on the breath to build some concentration and then turn your mind to your question, bringing to bear your intuition as well as your reason. Sometimes answers appear from a deeper level of your being when you reflect in a focused state in this way. If you don't get anywhere through meditative reflection and the issue is still there like a fallen tree blocking your progress, you need to find someone who can help you to reach satisfactory answers. Here you really do need contact with a meditation group or teacher.

The most common form of doubt for Westerners is probably self-doubt. People tell themselves things like, 'Meditation may be wonderful, and I'm sure that other people gain excellent results from it, but it doesn't work for me. I'm not a meditator.' This often comes from having unrealistic expectations. On meditation courses I often hold one-to-one interviews. I frequently come across people who assume that everyone else is deeply concentrated and they are the only 'failure' whose concentration is patchy. If this sounds like you, then I promise you are not alone; most people find it difficult to stay aware. And there is no need to decide that you can't meditate. Anyone can do it. If you can keep your mind on the breath for at least three milliseconds then you have what it takes. You *can* deepen your awareness and your ability to concentrate. It is just a question of time, practice, and finding some self-belief.

If you find yourself with too much energy, too little, or afflicted by doubt, it is important not to make a problem of it. These are all just natural responses of the mind and everyone who meditates encounters them regularly. When you notice them, take them as useful information, signs from your mind of what it needs.

awareness mini-breaks

Being aware of the breath is not something that has to be limited to a 'meditation session'. Formal meditation is very valuable because it gives you the time to enter your experience more fully and undistractedly than usual. But you can gain some of the benefits of meditation by periodically returning to the breath for a few moments or minutes in the midst of your everyday life. So something else that I recommend is taking time out during the day for mini-meditations. Five minutes spent paying attention to the breath, or even two minutes in the middle of a busy day, all help to put you in touch with a deeper and calmer state of mind.

Waiting times are particularly good to use in this way: traffic jams, bus stops, station platforms, departure gates, or standing in line at the supermarket checkout. All these situations need no longer be 'wasted time'. Before I learned to meditate I would get bored when I had to 'hang around' and I would find some way of distracting myself. These days I can just turn to the breath and use the time to come closer to my experience rather than distracting myself and losing touch with it.

Travelling often provides useful opportunities to check in with the breath. I have had some good mini-meditations on the London Underground. I look at the map and count how many stations there are to my destination. Let's say there are five. I turn my attention to my breathing and start counting after the out-breath. When I feel the train stop and hear the doors open I move on to the second stage, and I move on another stage every time the doors open. In this way I finish the four-stage meditation at the fourth station, which gives me one more stop in which to stop meditating, open my eyes, and take in the adverts and the other passengers once again. Then I get up at my station, feeling brighter than when I sat down.

You don't even need a few minutes. These mini-breaks can be as short as a few seconds. You can try to become aware of two or three breaths when you switch activities, such as when you stop for a drink, while your computer boots up, or before you answer the phone. We are often propelled through the day from one activity to another from the moment the alarm rings, and we never manage to catch our breath. Just a few moments in which you stop, come to your senses, and feel the breath of life flowing into your body make a real difference. In my early years of meditation I worked as a social worker for a local authority. Like all such agencies, our department was avalanched with work. I trained myself to stop and take a couple of breaths whenever I picked up a case file. Not only was it a couple of seconds of peace in the bedlam of a busy office, it was a useful prompt to keep the initiative, a reminder that moment by moment I always had a choice about how I was living.

So do try giving yourself short breaks in which you touch base with your breath. You could take one right now, before you read the next paragraph.

You don't need to be sitting down to do this. You can practise awareness of the breath while walking. In that situation it doesn't really work to focus completely on the breath or you may start walking into trees or lampposts. Instead, you simply use awareness of the breath as a way of helping you to be present in your body, in the here and now, as you walk along. Using the terms we looked at earlier, you keep your awareness quite broad, with just some focus. You will often find that the breath falls into a rhythm with your movement, so that you are taking a certain number of paces with each breath. That natural rhythm often helps your concentration.

So there are lots of possibilities for using the breath to calm and centre yourself during the day. However, except in an emergency, it isn't helpful to use these mini-meditations as a substitute for a regular, longer period of practice. Use them in addition to it, as boosters to heighten your awareness.

4

beginning and ending well

Most successful events in life are born from the right preparation. For example, if you are going to drive somewhere you usually do a number of things, almost as second nature, before you set the wheels spinning. If you weren't the last person to use the car, you check that the seat is in the right position for you, and that the mirrors give you a clear view of what is happening behind you. You also glance at the gauges to make sure that you have enough fuel and that everything is in order. You do all this before heading off because you know that it is time well spent, and will give you the best chance of getting to your destination safely and smoothly.

preparing to meditate

Although I saw the value of preparation in situations like driving, for a long time I didn't believe in spending time on it before meditation. If I was going to meditate on the breath I would sit down, quickly adjust my posture, and then immediately go hunting for the sensations of my breathing. I would listen to meditation teachers suggesting a more structured approach to preparation and then just ignore them. Some of the time, if I was highly motivated and raring to go, I would get away with it. But it eventually dawned on me that frequently what I thought of as my keenness to meditate was just impatience. And often, because I hadn't prepared well, hadn't made a proper start, and hadn't really committed myself to the meditation, my mind would quickly drift away to whatever it was currently preoccupied with and only wander back to the breath when it was almost time to finish the practice.

So I learned from experience that a few minutes spent preparing weren't a waste of valuable time that could have been spent on the 'real meditation'. Diving straight in wasn't usually the quickest way to enter a meditative state of mind. Good preparations set up the conditions for the whole meditation to go well. So in this chapter we'll look at ways of preparing that will give you the best chance of arriving at a state of relaxation and heightened awareness. And at the end of the chapter we'll talk about how you can emerge from meditation well-prepared for the next activity of your day.

Having tried to ignore it for years myself, I now believe that preparing well is one of the most effective ways to improve your meditation practice. A good preparation routine helps you make the transition from everyday life to meditation. It puts you in touch with the breadth of your experience – with who you are and where you are – which gives you a supportive context in which to focus on the breath.

It also strikes me that many of the difficulties that people have with meditation stem from lack of preparation. If you don't prepare yourself physically before you start, you are more likely to be uncomfortable during the practice. If you don't prepare mentally, you may not make a connection with your sense of purpose, and when you don't know why you're meditating it usually doesn't go well. So, like driving, preparations for meditation fall into two main categories. There are the ones that are more immediate and physical, that lead directly into the experience; then there are the mental ones that are all about knowing where to go and how to get there.

preparing physically
setting up your meditation posture
Physical preparation begins with checking and adjusting your physical posture. You want to find a position that allows you to be relaxed and comfortable but also alert and with a clear sense of what is going on. Meditation is also a blend of relaxation and awareness, with the emphasis on awareness. So you need to find a position in which you are alert and in which you can stay comfortably without moving for a reasonable length of time.

It's possible to meditate on the breath when walking, standing, or even lying down (though with the latter you may just drift off to sleep). But the classic posture for meditation is sitting. To achieve this balance of letting go and being vividly present, the main requirement is that you sit with your spine straight but not rigid. You can do this in various ways.

sitting cross-legged on cushions on the floor

kneeling supported by a stool or a pile of cushions

sitting on a straight-backed chair with your feet planted firmly on the ground

Any of these postures will give you a solid base out of which your spine can rise up, so that there is a sense of creating space between the vertebrae. In this way you avoid the two extremes. If your spine is ramrod, 'sergeant major' straight you will not be able to relax. If it is slumped and not extending upwards you will lose awareness and a sense of aliveness in the meditation.

Once you are seated with your back straight, there are several other points that most people find helpful.

1. Let your *head* move slightly forward and up from the neck, then very slightly tuck in your chin. (The position of your head and neck is decisive for what happens with your posture.)

2. Allow your *neck* to be soft, and your *shoulders* to sink downwards, but don't slump forwards.

3. Rest your *tongue* on the roof of your mouth, a little way behind your front teeth.

4. Your *hands* can rest in your lap or out on your thighs. If they are in your lap you may find it helpful to support them, perhaps with a cushion which helps to take the weight of your arms.

5. Your *eyes* can be closed or half open, with your gaze resting unfocused a few feet ahead of you.

Meditation posture is something about which you could write a booklet – and indeed people have (see the *Further Reading* section for a recommendation). It is very good if you can have someone qualified check your posture from time to time to suggest improvements. Otherwise you will not gain the full reward from your work in meditation. There are certain unhelpful habits that you can get into, like slumping in the lower back, or letting your chest cave in, which are the equivalent of driving with the handbrake on: they put a drag on the practice, making it hard for your energy to flow into the meditation. Or you might be pushing your chest forward and lifting your head in a way that is the meditational equivalent of revving in neutral – feeding too much energy into the practice and causing unnecessary strain and tension.

After you have been practising for a while, you will find a natural posture that supports your meditation.

You will probably notice that the posture in which it is easiest to meditate is also one that enables you to breathe easily and naturally. Once you have the experience to know how a good posture feels – grounded, relaxed, and full of vitality – it will only take you a minute at the beginning of the meditation to tune in to what is going on and make any necessary adjustments.

preparing mentally
tuning in to your sense of purpose
To achieve anything in life other than drifting along the line of least resistance – which would leave most of us slumped in front of the TV – you need to be motivated. As we saw in the last chapter, without enjoyment, interest, and keeping in touch with your reasons for doing it, your meditation will be very hit-and-miss. Of those three, a sense of purpose is the most fundamental, so before you begin your work with the breath it is very important to spend a minute or two getting in touch with the reasons for doing it, the things that generate some enthusiasm in you. What inspires you to meditate today? Why are you sitting down to spend this time with yourself? Your reasons for meditating may be different on different days and will almost certainly change over time as your experience of meditation deepens. In order to engage your energy with the practice, you may call to mind things that generally motivate or inspire you, or you may find some that are specific to that particular session.

Examples of general reasons for meditating could be:

I want to become calmer and kinder.

Meditation helps me to feel less stressed.

It would be really good to deepen my ability to concentrate.

I want to understand the meaning of life.

Specific motivations for a particular meditation could be:

I have a difficult meeting this morning. Some time spent on my meditation cushion will help me deal with it more creatively.

In my last meditation I felt a sense of something releasing deep inside me and I was very contented. I know you can never have exactly the same experience twice, but if I can relax into the breath again then that process of tension release can continue.

The violence and suffering that I saw on that news bulletin last night were horrendous. I may not be able to do anything to help directly but I can use it to encourage me to work to become a more peaceful and effective human being. Then at least I can have a positive influence on the people that I meet.

preparing mentally
reviewing what you will be doing
If you are new to meditation on the breath, once you have found a sense of purpose the next step is to call to mind the method, so that you are clear about how you are going to meditate. For instance, if you learn and use the four-stage approach to concentrating on the breath suggested in Chapter 2, then at the beginning of the meditation you would mentally review the four stages and any advice on how to use them that you have found helpful. This is the equivalent of checking the map before you set out to drive somewhere. Of course, after a while the meditation method becomes second nature, like following a route you have travelled many times before, and there is no need to prepare in this way. However, you might still spend a few moments recalling your recent meditations and things that helped you to take them deeper, so that you are prepared if similar opportunities arise during the coming practice.

preparing mentally
checking your internal state
Even though you have travelled the same road many times before, the conditions will never be quite the same on any two journeys. So you may check the weather forecast and a traffic bulletin in order to see what you will be up against en route. Similarly, before you launch into the actual meditation it is very helpful to tune in to how you are feeling. You turn your attention inwards and take a sounding of your state, sense your own internal weather conditions. How are you feeling right now? What is the quality of your

thoughts? Are they light and bright, or circling constantly around something that you have on your mind? How is your energy? Do you have a full tank or are you running on empty? In this way you are establishing a broad awareness prior to focusing on the breath.

This period of tuning in to how you are is a helpful preparation for meditation in two ways. First, it gives you useful information about the kind of conditions you will be working with during the meditation. For example, if your mind is turning over some problem, you are likely to feel the gravitational pull of that during the meditation. So you can prepare yourself to work with that if it happens, reminding yourself not to get caught up with it. (You might even reflect on it briefly and set aside some time when you will give the problem your full attention, perhaps later in the day or straight after the meditation when your mind will be clearer.) If you notice you are feeling energetic but restless, you can prepare yourself to work on calmness and relaxation.

Secondly, this period of listening to yourself is already the beginnings of meditation. All meditation involves engaging with your experience, developing a subtle awareness of yourself as a living being in the present moment. If you listen to your feelings in this way it is excellent preparation for tuning into the sensations of the breath during the actual meditation.

preparing physically
doing a body scan

As a final preparation, it is good to bring your awareness back to your body and to spend time experiencing it bit by bit. This helps you to get in touch with your physical experienc,e and to prepare for the deep relaxation of the meditation, by bringing into awareness any areas of physical tension and gently working at letting them go.

You can scan through your body in two ways, either starting with the crown of your head and working downwards or starting from the soles of your feet and working upwards. For most people, the first is more effective. But if you are feeling tired, dull, or low, you may find that it works better to bring energy up the body by moving upwards to your crown. (You will come to notice as you become proficient in meditation that your awareness leads your energy. So if you concentrate on a particular place in your body, energy will accumulate there.)

So if you start from your crown, you begin by feeling the sensations of your scalp and then work down to your forehead, eyes, ears, and the back of your head. Then you carry on to your neck and throat and so on through your body.

It's possible to do all this body awareness purely from your head, as though you were a passive observer of the scan, but this isn't what it's about. You don't want your mind to be dissociated from your experience, like some space probe orbiting one of Jupiter's moons and collecting data. You need to be *in* the experience.

It's important to gain a feeling for these two kinds of awareness – passive observing and being in the experience. To do this, as you're reading you might like to experiment with two ways (or two ends of a spectrum of ways) in which you can experience your right hand. In one, your hand is that object on the end of your arm. You can see it down there and feel it sending messages to Central Control in your head. In the other, your hand is something that you experience from inside. You put your awareness into it and directly feel the bones, the muscles and skin, the temperature of the palm and the back of the hand, the life and energy that flow through it.

When you do the body scan, you move down the body in this engaged way, putting yourself into one part after another, noticing any tension and letting it go, until you are in your feet with all their bones and nerve endings. Once you have scanned through the different parts of your body, spend a few moments gaining an overall sense of it. Then turn your attention to your breathing and begin the meditation.

We have just explored *five stages of preparation:*

> *setting up your posture*
>
> *tuning into your sense of purpose*
>
> *reviewing what you are going to do*

checking your internal state

doing a body scan

All this detail makes them appear to involve a lot of work, but they quickly become second nature. It can be well worth spending a few minutes on the body scan, so that you are strongly grounded in your physical experience before you turn to the breath. But the others needn't take long at all and they are time well spent, even if brief. Like driving, it is worth setting up good habits, otherwise you're likely to fall into bad ones. After all, as you discover with practice, meditation has its equivalents of getting completely lost, snarled up in traffic, or running out of fuel. It is well worth spending a few minutes to avoid these pitfalls.

preparing to leave the meditation
Meditation is an altered state of consciousness. As we've seen, it requires certain preparations. The same is true for going the other way, from meditation back into everyday life. So we'll take a little time now to look at how to end a meditation session well – otherwise it would be like teaching you to drive without giving you any lessons in stopping or parking.

In leaving the meditative state there are three main things you are trying to achieve:

to make the mental transition from inner to outer experience
In meditation on the breath you are using your mind in a particular way. You are focusing strongly on one

object of concentration. As you do so, your percep-
tions of the outer world – sights, sounds, and so on –
move to the periphery of your attention. Also your
mind's tendency to follow one train of thought after
another is reduced. All this is restful and energizing.
However, in everyday life you need to be fully in
your senses, and to think about what you are doing.
So at the end of a meditation session you need to
make sure that you have fully arrived back in your
senses and your brain is in the right gear for your next
activity.

to carry over the benefits from the meditation into your everyday life

Although you need to make a transition at the end of
meditation to using your mind in a different way, you
don't want to lose touch with the positive effects of
your session. Meditation generates awareness, calmness, and other benefits. These have very positive
effects on your mind. However, our experience is
often very compartmentalized. When we are in one
mental state, it is easy to lose touch with what happened in another one. For instance, you may have a
very moving and vivid dream but then find that it
quickly fades away as you become engaged with your
day. So to gain the maximum benefit from meditation
you need to make the transition into everyday life as
seamless as possible, so that you carry over the beneficial effects of the meditation into your activities.

to re-engage the body

If you become deeply concentrated in meditation,
your body will become extremely relaxed. It can feel

like a cat that has been lying in front of a fire. You try to make it stir but it feels completely heavy and boneless. So you need to gently stretch and move it so that it is ready to move into activity again.

leaving the meditation

To achieve these three goals, it is good to go through a routine like the one below when you come to the end of a session of meditating on the breath.

1. *Widen out your awareness* from the breath to include the rest of your body.

2. *Take note of your mental and emotional states*. Notice how these have changed from when you sat down to meditate. Take time to assimilate them. Savour any positive changes that you notice.

3. *Bring your attention back to your body* and begin to move it very gently in a way that feels right to you. I often begin by moving my head a bit, first down towards one shoulder then the other. Then I swing my whole torso a little to right and left. After that I slowly move my hands, bringing energy back into them.

4. If you have been meditating with *your eyes* closed then *gently open* them. Or if you have had them half closed, open them fully and focus them again.

5. *Take in your surroundings*, the sights and sounds around you.

6. *Move the body* a little more vigorously, and disengage your legs if you have been seated cross-legged or kneeling.

7. *When you are ready*, get up, stretch a little, and then *move on* to your next activity.

Don't skip this routine, even if you think your meditation was not very concentrated. It isn't always easy to judge the depth of your absorption. Sometimes in meditation you may feel as if your mind was all over the place and then be surprised when you try to leap up and move on to the next activity – it's a shock to your system. So it never does any harm to give yourself time at the end.

Very occasionally you may find that even after you have gone through these steps you feel a little strange – as if part of you is still in the meditation and you are not fully present in your experience. If this happens to you, it is just a sign that you did not take long enough to come out of the meditation. It is nothing to worry about. The answer is simple: close your eyes, take your attention inwards again for a little while, then emerge very slowly and consciously. It is like deep-sea divers who come up from a dive too fast and get the bends: they need to go back down to a depth at which they are comfortable and then come up gradually to give themselves time to readjust to the surface pressure.

Ideally, it is good if you can give yourself a period of undemanding activity after meditation. Make a drink, walk the dog, or sit and look out the window for five minutes: anything that allows you to stay fairly close to the meditative experience of doing one thing fully and with awareness makes a good bridge between meditation and the full-on demands of everyday life.

5

the story you tell yourself

As you live your life, you describe it to yourself. In effect, you tell yourself a story about who you are and how things are going. So someone who is asked to introduce themselves might say, 'I'm Joan. I'm 42 years old, married with two daughters. I work as a pharmacist, which I enjoy. But I'm worried at the moment because my youngest daughter doesn't seem interested in going to college.' In this way people tell you part of the story of how they see their lives. Naturally we carry this tendency into meditation. After we have been practising for a while we have a whole story about ourselves as a meditator: 'I'm Tom. I've been meditating fairly regularly for about three months now. I took it up because my work is very stressful and I thought it might help. I do have days when it goes well, and my mind becomes quieter. But often my head is full of to-do lists and I can't find the breath at all. Maybe I'm not cut out to be a meditator.'

Having watched many people take up this practice, I've come to see that the story you tell yourself – about how you are doing and where you are heading with meditation – crucially conditions what you get out of it. So in this chapter we'll look at some of the elements of that story: some of the views and attitudes that you may bring to the meditation. We'll look at some that get in the way of your practice, and some that are helpful and supportive.

'good' and 'bad' meditation
After you have been meditating for a while, you inevitably begin to make judgements about how it is going. Many of these are unhelpful, and arise from a misunderstanding of what meditation is about. This is particularly risky for us in the West, where we are often very perfectionist about things, expecting ourselves to be able to 'do it right' (whatever 'it' is) from the beginning. If you have mistaken ideas of what makes a good meditation, and then insist that you live up to that wrong idea, you have a recipe for failure and very unpleasurable meditation.

In my early years of practice I thought I knew what good and bad meditations were. I assumed that a good meditation was one in which I managed to stay concentrated on the breath and in which I experienced happy, buoyant states of mind. A bad meditation was one in which my mind wandered or I was too dozy to pay attention. While this is true from an ideal point of view, I now recognize that seeing things in that way was very unhelpful. These days I think very little about 'good' and 'bad' in relation to meditation. On the contrary, meditation can give us a respite from the frequent tendency of our mind to judge and compare, and especially to find ourselves lacking and run ourselves down.

When I do think in such terms these days, I judge a good meditation to be one in which I make a gentle, steady effort to improve my mental state: to develop awareness, to channel my energy away from memories, daydreams, and repetitive thinking, and lead it into the here and now, into the experience of being alive to the breath. A bad meditation is one in which I don't get around to making that gentle, steady effort.

In meditation you are learning all the time about the different states your mind gets into. One of the things you see early on is that the mind is made up of a continuous stream of different mental states. Some are happy, some are sad. Some are peaceful, some are restless. That is just human nature. What is important is that through meditation you can improve the trend of those states and make them increasingly fulfilling. It's the effort that you make in each meditation – to stay aware and, if possible, leave your mind better than you found it – that is important. So you might sit down one day and feel already quite peaceful and concentrated, and make no effort to take those states further. That would be a bad meditation. On another day you could sit down to find yourself restless, bored, and irritated. But rather than blanking out, you could stay aware of what was going on. Bit by bit you could use gentle persistence to keep leading your reluctant mind back to the breath. At the end of the meditation you still might not feel wonderful, but you would have done useful work in leading your emotions in a positive direction. That would be a good meditation.

So don't judge your meditation by the feelings that you find, or by your level of concentration. The only useful yardstick is whether you made an effort to stay aware and stay with the breath. If you did that, you can congratulate yourself. The effort will have left its mark on your mind. If you keep making a gentle effort to lead your mind to the breath, you will find the quality of your mental states improving over time. Through the positive efforts you are making, you are catalysing deep changes in your mind.

helpful and unhelpful attitudes

In this section we'll look at some issues that I had to learn about the hard way. After I had been meditating on the breath for a year or so, I began to take part in the meditation days that were regularly held in that former piano factory. These involved a lot of forty- or fifty-minute periods of meditation. Each time I would start off full of determination to go deeply into meditation, and sometimes I had a bit of initial success. But as the day wore on I would become increasingly tense. My mind would refuse to cooperate in staying with the breath, engaging defiantly (or so it felt) with anything else but what I was asking it to do. By mid-afternoon I would have a lot of tension in my shoulders and the beginnings of a headache. By the end I'd be feeling as if I'd have a better chance of making a piano than of ever counting as far as ten breaths.

So what was happening? Essentially I was making the wrong kind of effort, based on an incorrect idea of how to concentrate. My images of concentration were all of forcing my mind to do something it didn't want to do. At school, my science teachers would yell 'Concentrate!' at me, and I would pull my mind back to some set of equations or formulae that I wasn't interested in because nobody had shown me their relevance to the real world. My school was in Wimbledon, and in the summer I would go to watch the tennis. There I saw players psyching themselves up at crucial moments, fists clenched, talking to themselves, cursing when they missed a shot.

From these experiences my model of concentration involved forcing myself, using a lot of will-power, to achieve a goal that I had set myself. To achieve the result I wanted I would try to bring as much energy to bear on the task as possible. When my mind refused to cooperate, I would drag it back, like a truanting schoolkid being taken to see the head teacher, lecture it, and try to force it to stay put. Operating like that, it was not surprising that I ended up with a headache.

Yet, if I'd thought about it, I had a whole different set of experiences of concentration that I could have drawn on when I was learning to meditate. I could become completely absorbed in a good book, playing soccer, or watching the waves breaking on the rocks during seaside holidays. In those situations I never had to force myself at all; my mind became naturally engrossed in what I was experiencing.

So from all this I learned some lessons.

meditation depends on enjoyment, interest, and a strong sense of purpose

I know we talked about these earlier, but I want to mention them again to remind you (and myself). These really are crucial, and trying to force yourself to concentrate is a sure sign that they are missing. If you manage to line up all three together, you are almost guaranteed to hit the jackpot in meditation.

focusing on results doesn't work

In those day-long sessions I was highly motivated to meditate – otherwise I wouldn't have kept putting myself through such misery. I really wanted to experience higher states of consciousness, bliss, enlightenment, and all those other wonderful fruits of meditation that I had heard about. However, although such motivations may be helpful to get you into meditation (particularly if they're backed up by some that are more specific and immediate), once you engage with a session of practice you have to put them all down and focus on the process, on what's under your nose (literally, in the fourth stage).

you need to treat yourself as a living being

That may sound like stating the glaringly obvious, but I know that my approach to difficulties in meditation was often like fixing some machine that had stopped working at an inconvenient moment. I would take a crude approach to it and try to find a fix, a technique, some quick way of manipulating my mind into working in the way I wanted it to. But as human beings, we are life. We are wondrous, complex, growing, living organisms. As you meditate it becomes clear over the years just how rich and amazing our consciousness is. So we need to treat ourselves with respect, care, love, attention, and subtlety. I would never treat a plant in the way I treated myself in my early years of meditation. I was doing the equivalent of noticing that a plant was starting to wilt and trying to wrench it upright again. But a real plant I observe carefully, and think about the conditions it needs in order to grow happily: what sunlight, water, and nutrients can I give it? The same is true for us. In meditation we need to stay aware of how we are responding to changing conditions, and make sensitive adjustments.

make friends with yourself

In my early times of meditation there was constant tension between me 'here' and my mind 'over there', which was not doing what I wanted it to do. It was stubborn, pig-headed, perverse. No sooner had I got it nicely focused on the breath than it would go chasing some old pop tune that I'd never liked anyway. We were like a pair of bickering lovers – tied together but constantly having rows. The same would happen with my body. I would feel I was doing well with the meditation until my knee started to hurt, my leg went numb, or I got an infuriating itch somewhere.

The whole relationship between 'mind', 'body', and 'you' is a very mysterious one that Buddhism has investigated deeply. For now, it's enough to notice that when you're happy, relaxed, and focused you don't feel a big separation between the body or mind and you. If I give an old friend a hug, I don't think, 'My body did that really well.' And when I'm engrossed in a film, I don't notice my 'mind' at all. But when things aren't going how I want in meditation, I feel my mind and body as objects, separate from me. So I think, 'I could meditate really well now if my ankle wasn't hurting,' or, 'My mind won't settle down at all this morning.'

Whenever you notice yourself feeling emotionally distanced from what is going on in your meditation, the secret is to turn towards your experience. Open yourself to what is happening. To start with, you could lighten up around it, take a friendly interest in it. After all, it is part of your experience of life. Fundamentally, our attitude to ourselves and all our experience in meditation needs to be as kind and open-hearted as we can make it. That doesn't mean giving up on the breath and just following that old pop tune. It means that the attitude with which we work with ourselves needs to be as open and loving as possible. Working with difficulties in meditation can be a bit like persuading a child to do something that you know will benefit it. Like a child, your body and mind don't usually respond well to being ordered around. In meditation, as with parenting, love and friendly encouragement achieve far more than 'Do as I say!'

In this chapter we've looked at some of the helpful and unhelpful things you can tell yourself. The best approach to meditation would be to have no story at all. Then you would have real 'beginner's mind': no expectations of yourself or the meditation, just doing it and seeing what happens. For that very reason many people have a good experience of meditation the first time they try it. They sit down with no expectations and just follow the instructions. But that first experience then starts them talking to themselves: 'Hey, this meditation's great. I want it always to be like that,' which gets in the way. So, given that we can't completely avoid building up views and opinions, the best one would be something like, 'I don't have to be anything special as a meditator. Anyone can explore their experience and work at becoming more aware, so that's what I'm doing. I don't expect miracles, but I trust that meditation is a process of learning and it unfolds over time. So I don't get too carried away when it goes well, and on days when I'm all over the place I don't give myself a hard time.' If there is a secret to meditation, it's to put all your expectations, good or bad, to one side, and come back to this breath, now – and trust that process.

6

deepening the meditation

blending the mind with the breath

A lot of the time we human beings live our lives on autopilot. This is natural, as our mind tries to help us out by dealing with a lot of things automatically – for instance, we don't usually need to pay attention to how we move our arms when we walk – so that we are free to focus on what we feel is important. One of the ways in which it does this is by using a kind of mental shorthand. It gives us an idea about something, or a symbol for something, to save us having to deal with the complexity of the actual experience. For example, suppose you are late for a meeting in an unfamiliar town and have been told that the place you want is just past the post office. When you come to the post office your mind doesn't bother you with all the actual details of the building: the design of the windows or the sunlight playing on the roof. You recognize the symbol for the post office, use it as a signpost, and hurry on to your meeting. This ability of the mind to filter our experience is very useful, but the problem is that we can't always find the off switch – our mind carries on producing ideas about things when we really want the full, direct experience.

This tends to happen when you first work with the breath in meditation. You often find that you are not actually in the rich stream of experience that is the breath. Instead, you are meditating on a subtle idea *about* the breath, how you imagine it is or how it ought to be, rather than having a direct encounter with the physical reality of it. None of this is bad; the mind's capacity to distance itself from experience is useful. But when you meditate on the breath you are working to feel it directly, to become intimate with it, and with all the subtle changes that occur within it moment by moment.

When you notice that the breath is not very vivid, that your experience of it is thin, or that your mind is presenting you with an idea about it, you need to work slowly to bring your awareness more into your body. Once you are more grounded, you can gently bring your attention to the details of the breath itself, such as the muscles involved in the rise and fall of the abdomen, the way in which the air seems to flow more strongly in one nostril than the other, or how the breath affects the energy flow in your whole body. As your practice deepens all this will happen naturally, but you can encourage it through awareness.

unusual physical experiences

As you start to become more concentrated on the breath, you may find you experience odd physical sensations. In my early days of practice I used to find at times that my body felt enormous, cathedral-like. At other times it would be hugely heavy, as if I was wearing a diving suit. Then again I would occasionally have the sensation that I somehow had a body within my physical body, and this inner body was slowly turning round, like a rotating restaurant, so that I would seem to be facing different directions. None of these sensations were unpleasant, and once I had been reassured that they were normal I quite welcomed them, as they gave me a sense that something was happening.

There are different theories about what causes these experiences. They don't usually arise once you are deeply concentrated; they are generally a sign that your concentration is starting to deepen. Some people suggest they are brought about by subtle energy imbalances. Another view is that they happen as you make the transition from working with a mental construct of the body and breath to a more direct experience of them. Your body-image breaks down as you widen your awareness and new information floods in from your senses.

So if you experience these unusual sensations just take them as a sign that your concentration is starting to deepen. Stay with the breath and they will open out into richer and more satisfying experiences.

If you have this kind of experience in a meditation it is important to make sure that you end that session slowly. Gently withdraw your attention from the breath and give yourself time to feel fully back in the room and grounded in your body. Then take your time before you open your eyes. If you find the experiences are continuing – a rare event but possible – take yourself back into the meditation and re-emerge more slowly. You have been in a different world; give yourself more time for your mind and energy to adjust to the change in consciousness.

varying the count

When teaching this meditation I usually recommend that people work with the four-stage method for some time. As we've seen, it can be very helpful for your mind to have a format to work with, and this is designed to help your concentration to become more refined as you move through the stages. In this way your mind learns a positive habit, which to start with often makes the meditation easier. However, as with many things in life, what starts out being a positive habit may turn into an unhelpful rut. What helped you to stay alive to your experience can become another way of putting yourself on autopilot.

So, after you have established your meditation practice, it is important to keep checking to see if the four-stage approach is still a help rather than a boring old script. Does it encourage you to be more alive in your experience, or is it now a barrier to becoming one with the breath?

To start with, if the latter is the case, it can be helpful to retain the four stages but use your own judgement about how long to spend on each one. So if your concentration is rather weak one day, you might spend the majority of your time in the first stage, gaining the benefit of the counting to help you to stay with the breath. On another day you might find you become concentrated quite quickly, so you can pass rapidly through the first two or even three stages and dive happily into the last stage. Or you might be in stage three of a practice and realize that you need the support of the counting and revert to stage two. In this way you can use the four stages as tools rather than seeing them as set in stone.

As time goes on, you may want to experiment with counting to different numbers. What happens if you only count to five? Or if you go on to twenty-one rather than ten? What if you just keep on counting, higher and higher, throughout the first two stages? What happens if you visualize the numbers rather than hearing them? Or if you say them loudly to yourself, or very quietly? All these will have subtly different effects on your mind. While you don't want to make the practice too gimmicky, it is always interesting to experiment and see what you learn.

In some respects, meditation is like learning any other skill. Let's go back to my driving analogy. When you're learning to drive your instructor gives you clear procedures to follow: 'mirror, signal, manoeuvre', or whatever. You go out for practice runs along roads you will not find too taxing. But once you have passed your test you may find your own ways of doing things. Some of what you were taught will have become second nature, some you may want to question: 'Why do it like that? What happens if I do it like this?' You become more autonomous, and can go off exploring all kinds of interesting side roads. Some of this experimentation may lead to painful experience. Your decision to experiment with turning before signalling may lead to some close calls and being surrounded by angry horns; your exploration off the beaten track may take you down blind alleys or into a dangerous neighbourhood. But you can still learn from these mistakes, and often you learn in a much deeper way than if you simply follow what it says in the manuals.

So feel free to try things out. Learn from your experience what happens if you count differently. Or you could experiment with replacing the count with words or short phrases. For instance, a friend of mine who finds she is often quite tense says things like 'calm' and 'relax' to mark her breaths. Or you could keep it simple and just use 'in' and 'out' on your inhalation and exhalation.

letting go of the four stages
You can also experiment with dropping the four stages altogether and keeping one focus throughout your meditation time. You could just do the third or even the fourth stage. You don't have the same advantages of a structured approach for deepening your concentration, but on the plus side you don't

disturb your mind by changing your object of concentration every few minutes.

Most people's minds are restless by nature and there are two approaches you can take to this. The four-stage method accommodates itself to this tendency. It is like giving a frisky animal a large field to romp around in to start with, and gradually leading it to a single point as it tires of wandering around. The stages provide your jumpy mind with a series of tasks that are graded so that, as it starts to settle, it is given something to do that requires greater stillness and steadiness of concentration.

Some people prefer a much more uncompromising approach. They feel that giving an animal too large a field just encourages it to keep roaming around, getting stirred up by the different sights, sounds, and smells. Rather than trying to lead the mind gently in the right direction, it should be given strong medicine. The antidote to restlessness is to tether the mind to one point until it becomes used to staying still.

If the latter approach appeals to you, or if you find the counting has become very mechanical and is no longer a help, then by all means try out the 'one-stage method'. Take the third or fourth stage and work with it exclusively. In fact you can take this approach with any of the stages. If the counting works well for you, you could experiment with using just the first or second stage.

exploring the breath in the body
Another whole area to explore is where in the body you focus on the breath. In the third and fourth stages you concentrate on following the breath down into the lungs and back, and then on the area around the upper lip or just inside the nostrils. But there are several other ways of focusing on the breath in the body.

1. *the abdomen*
One traditional method of practice is to bring your attention to the way in which your abdomen rises and falls as you breathe. If you are breathing healthily, the in-breath should push the abdomen outwards, and then with the out-breath it should move inwards. You simply feel this movement, moment by moment.

It is worth noting at this point that the Western obsession with having a flat, hard stomach, or a six-pack, is not very helpful from the meditative point of view. Chronic holding-in of the abdomen prevents your diaphragm going through a full range of movement and doesn't allow the breath to find a natural, relaxed rhythm. So in focusing on the abdomen it is important to allow the belly to become soft, so that the breath can work its magic unobstructed by tension in that area.

2. *the hara*
In Zen Buddhism, and some other forms of Buddhist practice, the point of concentration in the abdominal area is specified much more precisely. There is said to be a point in the body a little below the navel, about

four finger widths lower down, which is an important centre of awareness. This point is known in Japanese as the *hara*. Concentrating here gives a sense of being very anchored. It helps to draw energy away from the head, and therefore to quieten the constant traffic of thoughts that compete for attention with the experience of the breath. Focusing on the *hara* helps develop a very direct, flowing, spontaneous way of responding to the world.

3. *the whole body*

It can be interesting to scan the whole body to see how much of it is involved with the process of breathing. We tend to be aware of the front of our bodies and to neglect our backs. But the back of the body and all the ribs there are very directly involved in the breathing process. In fact, if you include the indirect effects of the breath in your awareness, you soon find that all of you participates in the breath. It is like a wave – both physical and energetic – that passes through your body and affects every part, from the crown of your head to your toes. Tracking the breath in this way can bring your whole body alive.

4. *breathing through your skin*

This is a further extension to feeling the wave of energy and movement that passes through your body as you breathe in and out through the nose. You can develop the feeling that your skin is permeable, taking in energy through every pore. You may not literally be able to feel this happening, but you can have a sense that with each breath all your pores are opening, that your body is drinking in life from the environment.

You can use visualization to help this process: you see the energy entering your body in the form of white or golden light. This is a very energizing way to practise and I mentioned it earlier as an antidote to sleepiness. It can also be very helpful if you are feeling low or depressed.

5. *breathing into tight places*
As you meditate, you will at times become aware of areas in your body where you are tense or tight. You can use the breath to help dissolve these knots away. Deliberately breathe into the constricted area. If it helps, you can imagine that the air is melting the tensions. When you do this, you may experience emotions associated with those locked-up areas of your body being released. You may find yourself angry, in tears, or laughing for no apparent reason. This is nothing to worry about. It's a good sign and shows that energy is being released. When strong emotions surface during the meditation, accept them as part of your experience. Keep a sympathetic and kind approach to what is happening. Allow the feelings to appear and then experience them fully, using the breath as an anchor so that you are not carried away by them. Then allow them to pass in their own time.

This kind of emotional work is a vital aspect of meditation. It frees up energy, and by letting go of feelings associated with past hurts and traumas you will find yourself living much more fully in the present moment.

A large part of this chapter has been about suggesting ways in which you could experiment with breath meditation. That does raise the questions of how far and how soon it is helpful to do this. Certainly there needs to be some structure to your practice. It provides a kind of steady rhythm, like a heartbeat, linking all your meditation experience together. But one person's structure is another's straitjacket, so it is one of those questions which you can't really answer in the abstract. It is an area in which it is much easier to be working with a teacher or meditation group where you can receive advice and guidance. If you are practising alone, you may need to experiment with how much to experiment. One thing is for sure. You will not explore all the depths of this practice in a few weeks, months, or years. In principle, you could take something like the four-stage method and use it indefinitely.

7

where the practice leads

While meditation is always about the here and now, it can be inspiring to look ahead and see where your practice can lead. I've been fortunate enough to meet quite a few men and women who have devoted their lives to meditation. I find these encounters fascinating. All human beings are complete worlds in themselves, but these meditators seem to be living in a very different world from most other people. They seem happy and fulfilled, as if they were in touch with some deep well of meaning and understanding. They have a lightness about them, an ease and playfulness. They are very present, and they seem to live to serve others – not in some martyrish way, but happily and naturally, taking care of someone else in the same way they would look after their own hands. Being with such people I am given a feeling that there is no end to the meditative journey, and that it leads to the heart of things – to freedom.

So to inspire ourselves and to help set the compass of our intuition to point in the right direction, we'll look in this chapter at ways in which meditation on the breath can develop over time. As with learning any skill, progress in meditation isn't a simple, linear development. You will find times when you reach a plateau and cannot climb beyond it, even times when you seem to be going backwards. Some people's progress is dramatic, with a number of 'big experiences'; others' is quiet and steady but just as effective.

being fully present in your body

Anyone who practises meditation on the breath for a while will notice that the process of bringing awareness to it gives you a heightened sense of being in your body. You feel the movements of your chest, ribcage, back, and abdomen much more fully and directly. This leads on to an enhanced feeling for the flow of energy in your body. As your awareness in meditation becomes more acute, you experience the breath energizing the body and the movements of energy that this produces. In this way you move from a sense of the body as a thing or possession that you have – which is most people's experience when they take up meditation – to a vivid, alive sense of being in your body and senses.

Becoming fully awake to your physical experience also brings you into the present moment. It puts a halt to the constant train of thoughts about past and future that so often run riot in our heads. It is surprisingly difficult to stay in the here and now. Our minds keep turning to unfinished business from the past or hopes, anxieties, and plans for the future. It can be a real relief to come back to the breath and the precious moment of experience that you are living right here, right now.

spaciousness and freedom to choose

Meditation doesn't just bring awareness to your physical experience. The effort to stay with the breath throws into sharp relief how your mind is working and your habitual mental patterns. As we've seen, this can be a bit of a shock at first, but as time goes on you realize that it is a definite gain. Knowing the ways your mind works – what catalyses difficult mental states and what helps you to dig yourself out of them – is a great advance in self-knowledge.

One of the greatest gifts of regular meditation is that it creates a mental spaciousness. This gives you a calm centre from which to operate in daily life. It also enables you to create a gap between stimulus and response in situations in which you would have re-acted blindly in the past. When someone annoys you, rather than losing your rag and saying something you know you will later regret, you catch yourself, come back to the breath for a moment, and make space to respond in a more creative way – perhaps just explaining in a calm way how their behaviour affects you, or putting yourself in their shoes and trying to understand their behaviour.

This mental space, this gap between stimulus and response, gives you more options, more freedom. Instead of being driven by habits and emotions you're hardly aware of, you can choose your responses much more. Thus meditation allows you to live a more considered, less driven life, and gives you the space in which to make choices that support your highest values.

a more awake life

After you have been meditating for some time, it dawns on you that meditation is affecting your life and that how you live your life is affecting your meditation. As meditation is fulfilling, it makes sense to try to bring your life into line with how you are during meditation. This involves making an effort to carry the kind of awareness that you produce in meditation through into your everyday life. This 'daily-life mindfulness' is a powerful way to transform yourself. It is a step up from the awareness mini-breaks that I suggested in Chapter 3.

Obviously you can't meditate off your chair or cushion in the way that you do on them. Trying to make breakfast or travel to work with your eyes closed and your mind focused on your breath is a short cut to disaster. However, you can work to keep aware during the day, living in the present moment and being awake to your experience. You can also keep up a background awareness of your breath. If you are performing simple tasks such as walking to the corner store or digging the garden then you can keep most of your attention on your breath. If you are engaged in activities that require your full attention, such as writing a letter or talking to a friend, you can bring your mind back to the breath from time to time.

In this way the breath becomes a kind of anchor, a way of touching base in the middle of a busy life. The calm that you gain from being aware of the breath will enable you to flow more peacefully through the day. When people around you are upset or flustered, you can come back to the breath, steady your mind, and have some calm and clarity to offer the situation. Although you may not be able to sit for formal meditation very much during the day, you will be practising a diluted form of meditation in all kinds of situations. This will also give a tremendous boost to your sitting meditation.

a change of heart
It is only fair to warn you that meditation will change you in all sorts of ways that you may not expect. Just as you become more alive to your senses, so that autumn colours may become more vivid and you can distinguish more shades, the same is likely to happen with your emotional life. The awareness the meditation generates will make you more sensitive to different tones of feeling: joy, anger, grief, contentment – the whole spectrum of human responses to life. That is a real benefit, but sometimes this opening of your heart may be very uncomfortable. It will inevitably throw into relief those times when you are keeping your heart closed to others. Just as you register the subtleties of an autumn leaf, you may notice more when an offhand remark of yours hurts a relative or friend, or your hurry to get to work gives you a short fuse with anyone who gets in your way.

I certainly found this happening to me after I had been meditating for a while. I started to feel uneasy about behaviour that I used not to think twice about. Previously, some people had just been pawns in the game of getting what I wanted. From a more open-hearted position they now became human beings just like me, whose feelings I had to take into account. For instance, I used to be a good card player. At college I would supplement my grant (this was back in the days when the British government still gave money to students rather than just loaning it to them) in all-night poker sessions. But once I began to meditate I couldn't bear to play for more than small change. I just didn't enjoy the pain I caused by relieving someone else of money that it hurt them to lose. I tried to tell myself they had chosen to play and that we all had the same theoretical chance of winning. But my open heart noticed that when I picked up the last of someone's chips at five in the morning, underneath the feeling of victory and success I didn't feel very good about myself. Stopping playing was inconvenient for me, both financially and because I enjoyed the excitement and skill of the game, but I knew I had to follow my heart.

So you may find that the meditation is prompting you to become more sensitive ethically, that your heart is opening to your friends, family, work acquaintances, and to the state of the world. Naturally, we resist this at times, but it is good to welcome it if you can. This deeper engagement with others and the state of the world will lead you out of the sense of isolation and alienation from life felt by so many people.

Meditating on the breath leads beyond itself, into reflecting on your life and how you want to live it, into a heartfelt engagement with the world around you. As following the breath leads you to follow your heart, you will feel much happier and more fulfilled as a human being.

According to the Buddhist tradition, this also works the other way around. If you live in an open-hearted and generous way, you will find it much easier to meditate. If you watch your responses closely, you will see that acting unethically gives you a sense of unease, of not being on good terms with yourself and the world. This unease stands in the way of deep concentration.

To promote this opening of the heart, meditation on the breath can be supplemented by another meditation that develops feelings of love and well-wishing for yourself and others.[8] This meditation on loving-kindness will be the subject of another volume in this series.

higher states of calm and concentration
If you practise this meditation regularly, you will find that, occasionally at least, you will become very focused on the breath. The Buddhist texts describe a number of stages of concentration that you can go

---

8 This meditation is known as the *mettā bhāvanā* in Pāli, or *maitrī bhāvanā* in Sanskrit. *Bhāvanā* means development. *Mettā*, or *maitrī*, means loving-kindness that knows no limits.

through. The good news is that not only are these states very concentrated, they are also very enjoyable. As you move through these stages of concentration you experience increasing fulfilment, traditionally described in the following ways:

happiness: This is a state in which you feel very joyful and at ease, on good terms with yourself and the universe.

tension release: Here the meditation loosens physical knots and tensions. This results in a release of energy, sometimes extremely powerful, which is experienced as delightful sensations such as tingling in the body and rapturous states of mind.

calm: This goes even further· than tension release. Once the physical tensions have been dissolved away you can move into an oceanic feeling of peace and tranquillity.

bliss: This calm leads on to a deep blissfulness, a depth of happiness that is pretty much inconceivable from the point of view of the everyday mind. It comes from a highly stable concentration.

Cultivating the higher levels of these states of concentration usually requires intensive practice and special conditions. It involves finding a place where you can be completely undistracted and devote yourself to meditation for a substantial period of time. Nonetheless, it is possible to have some tip of the tongue experiences of these states from time to time in your everyday practice. Even a taste of them will give you a new appreciation of the potential of your mind.

insight into the true nature of life
Although these states of calm and bliss are very enjoyable and deeply relaxing for the mind, they do not bring about any permanent transformation. You experience them for a few minutes, hours, or even longer, but then they fade. Within Buddhism that is not the ultimate aim; the ultimate aim is a permanent transformation of consciousness. Buddhism believes it is possible to see clearly the true nature of life, and that doing so can free us from the pains and frustrations that we all have as human beings. This is the Buddhist project, and surely it is the human project as well, Buddhist or not: to understand our existence so that it has true meaning. In order for that to happen you need to gain some direct, intuitive understanding (not just ideas but actual experience) of how things really are. You need to see the processes at work by which you create happiness or frustration for yourself.

Meditation on the breath helps us to experience the nature of existence in two ways. First, it acts to set up the conditions for us to reflect deeply on life's true nature. Usually, if we do get around to asking ourselves existential questions like 'Who am I?', we do so with a mental state that isn't up to the task. To find useful answers to such questions our minds need to be sharp, clear, and discerning. Meditating on the breath can give our mind those qualities. Otherwise we are trying to make out something in the dark with a fading torch. Through mindfulness of the breath we can bring all our energy into one bright, concentrated beam. With our mind in such a sharply focused state, we can then reflect deeply and see things clearly.

You can also use the breath itself as an object for discerning the nature of things. To do this you first need to build up a head of steam with concentration. Once your mind is steady and clear, you can begin to examine the characteristics of the breath, paying particular attention to the qualities that it has in common with all other phenomena. You can focus on how it constantly changes, watching as one breath fades away to be replaced by another in an unending chain. Or you can watch how it arises out of all kinds of conditions and only exists in dependence on those conditions. To pick a few major factors: in order to breathe you need at least one lung, a clear airway, and air at the right pressure. But once you begin to think about it you see that there is far more involved than this. And all those immediate conditions only exist because they in their turn are supported by a whole network of other conditions.

Again, you could focus on the 'I' that seems to be doing the breathing. When you examine your experience closely under the microscope of meditation, can you find this seemingly solid entity? Is there an unchanging 'me' having these experiences? Or is it actually just a ceaseless flow of thoughts, feelings, and sensations? What is the relationship between 'me' and the breath? Are they completely different? If so, how do they interact? Or are they the same, in which case how come you can distinguish them?

These questions are not intended to send you off into flights of philosophical speculation. Their aim is to make you curious about your experience so that you examine it more closely. We often take our basic view of the world for granted. For instance, we usually take it as given that there is an 'I' that stands separate from our experience, a person who can talk of 'my breath' as if it were a possession. The Buddhist analysis, using the kinds of questions I've outlined to explore actual experience, finds nothing fixed, no 'I' standing behind the flow of your experience. This may sound scary, but in Buddhism it is a very liberating insight, as we spend most of our lives at the service of this imagined 'I', like a mother bird ceaselessly feeding and caring for a cuckoo in her nest. Instead, once we see through this view we arrive at a place of freedom, we shed all our fears and anxieties, and we feel reconnected to the heart of life from which our false sense of 'I' had made us feel distanced.

Thus meditation on the breath can serve both as a way of sharpening the tools of insight into life's true nature and as the raw material from which insight meditation can learn its lessons.

the ānāpānasati sutta
A systematic approach to both calm and insight using meditation on the breath is given by the Buddha in a text called the *Ānāpānasati Sutta* – 'the text on mind-

fulness of breathing' – which is found in an early col-
lection of texts called the *Middle Length Discourses*.
The original is in Pāli, the canonical language of
South-East Asian Buddhism.[9] In this sutta the
Buddha outlines a complete path to realization based
on the breath.

He describes sixteen contemplations in four sets of
four. The first set focuses on the experience of the
breath in the body, the second on feelings, the third
on the mind, and the fourth on developing insight
into reality through seeing impermanence and letting go of attachments. In all these contemplations
the breath is used as a way of staying anchored in
your present experience.

This text demonstrates very clearly just how far meditating on your breath can take you. Focusing on the
breath is an excellent practice for those who are new
to Buddhist meditation, and it is also an excellent
practice for every stage of the journey of consciousness towards the state of radiant wisdom, compassion, and freedom that Buddhism calls
Enlightenment or Awakening.

For those who are committed Buddhists it can be inspiring to know that, according to some sources,
meditation on the breath is the practice in which the
Buddha was engaged at the time of his Awakening. (I

---

9 There are several translations of the *sutta* available in English. See
Further Reading for details of one by Larry Rosenberg.

have even seen it suggested that we take in so many molecules with each breath that, in all probability, with each one we are inhaling some molecules that were breathed in by the Buddha.) Even if you are un-decided about the value of Buddhism, it has always been happy for people to experiment with its meth-ods, to see in their own experience whether they work. The main thing is that you sit down and try meditating on the breath – not just once but over a period of time to give it a chance to work its magic.

8

the lessons of the breath

As I mentioned in the Introduction, I first learned to meditate on the breath in 1973. Over many years this meditation has been a faithful friend, giving me all kinds of helpful feedback and wise counsel. On a basic level it has given me useful criticism about how I was living my life – making me aware when I was putting myself under serious stress, while at the same time gently relaxing some of it away. It always told me the truth, even when I was so fixed on achieving some goal that I didn't want to listen. It helped me in situations when I was tense with anticipation – such as before a dental appointment, or as I waited to stand up to talk to a large hall full of people. On occasions it has laid out a banquet of bliss for me to enjoy.

Though I have certainly been grateful for all these gifts, what I have most appreciated in this old friend are the insights into life and how to live it that he or she (I'm not sure which) has given me. So in this final chapter I shall touch on some of the wise advice I have received from the practice. By doing this I don't want to prejudge what you may experience over time. I simply want to show you that this deceptively simple meditation contains all kinds of hidden depths and is worth befriending. You will be glad you made the effort and you will have a faithful companion for life, one who is always available to help you and mirror how you are.

I'm going to mention six discoveries that I have made through meditating on the breath, though that doesn't begin to exhaust what you can learn from it.

being pointed towards direct experience

It was only with hindsight that I realized something very interesting about being taught to meditate on the breath. It was the first thing that happened when I went to the Buddhist centre in North London. At the time, I did not question the fact that the Buddhist teaching began with meditation as it seemed a very natural place to start. But subsequently I began to think more about that first meditation class. I saw how significant it was that the first time I turned up I wasn't given a talk on Buddhism. I wasn't told about the Buddhist take on the meaning of life, or lectured to about Buddhist philosophy. Instead, they sat me down and asked me to come back to my experience, aside from all my ideas about it. Could I simply focus on the breath, on the fundamental experience of being alive?

In this way, I was pointed at the heart of Buddhism – and the heart of life. Buddhism acknowledges that your views about life are important, because they act as filters – rose-tinted or grey-tinted lenses through which you see yourself and the world. But it aims to get you away even from clear ideas *about* life and to wade out into the waters of actual experience. Otherwise you are like someone collecting travel brochures who never actually goes anywhere. You may know about all the different resorts and city breaks but you never explore a new shoreline, never walk the avenues and hear a different language.

Being awake, alive in your life, means encountering life directly, and not constantly filtering it through a set of ideas in your head. Meditating on the breath brings you into your body, into your senses, into a direct, vivid encounter with how things are.

learning the happiness of just breathing
Although I certainly didn't, and at times still don't, find this meditation easy, it has on occasions all happened in textbook fashion. There have been sessions in which I have steadily built up concentration so that by the end I have been perfectly poised on the subtle sensation of the air on the upper lip or inside the nostril. Those simple, subtle sensations have been completely satisfying and I have felt deep calm and bliss. And yet, as I often reflect when I have emerged from the meditation, all I was doing was breathing. It makes me laugh sometimes. In the everyday world I have a long shopping list of things that I need in order to feel happy and secure. My mind is constantly aiming to find or maintain a wish-list: a nice place to live, good friends, financial security, respect and appreciation, sexual fulfilment,

etc. And yet if I were to stop running through my life like some prize-winner given ten minutes to fill a supermarket trolley for free and instead to sit down and go deeply into the simplest of experiences, I would find all the happiness and contentment that I could want.

I forget, and keep having to remind myself, that my own body and mind can be the source of all the fulfilment I could ever wish for.

the art of not being in control
In my early days of meditating on the breath, I found it impossible not to control it in some way. I would relax and let it go – or so I thought. But as the months and years went by, I would keep discovering subtle ways in which I was still holding on, making it happen, pushing the river of the breath out of its natural course. On some deep level I didn't trust that things would work without my control and supervision. It took me a long time to learn that the meditation actually worked *better* if I let go and didn't interfere.

This lesson learned from the breath can be transferred into the rest of your life, and in two ways. First, there are many situations in which allowing your energy to flow naturally and spontaneously, uninhibited by preconceived ideas of how things ought to be, produces creative results. This is the spirit of Zen Buddhism, which values action that is unpremeditated and free. This is not the same as following the whims of the moment, thrown up by the surface of your mind. It comes from touching a level of consciousness in which you are deeply in touch with your direct experience, so that you act intuitively, with a swift certainty that outdistances the rational mind.

The second way in which the lesson comes in useful is about recognizing that life is out of our control. There are certainly many situations in which concerted action to achieve a goal is essential. All through the day I am choosing: muesli over cornflakes, awareness over mental drifting, working on this book rather than finding a last-minute flight to a Mediterranean beach. But all too often this ability to choose, to bring about my preferred outcome, hides from me the fact that ultimately life is not within my control. I cannot stop people dying in wars, terrorist attacks, or natural disasters, can't decide never to catch a cold, can't prevent my friends getting old, can't pencil in a sunny spring day in 2035 on which to die.

So the breath helps me to gather myself, to focus energy on changing what I can change. But it also teaches me to let go, to give in graciously, and allow the greater current of life to bear me on its journey.

everything changes

As you explore the breath, moment by moment, day by day, in meditation, you soon become aware that it is constantly changing. In a few seconds the in-breath transforms into the out-breath. After a few minutes of shallow breaths the rhythm changes and the intake of air becomes greater. Your mind that is experiencing the breath is also a river of changing states.

the breath

Everything comes to an end. A feeling of depression that had been squatting over your meditation, a heaviness that felt as if it had come to stay, finally dissolves away through patient effort. A peak meditation experience, filled with bliss and light, which feels as if it could never fade, slowly gives way to something more humdrum and everyday.

The breath is a wonderful teacher about the quicksilver, impermanent nature of … you name it. Living closely with the breath you learn not to hold on to good experiences but to savour them and let them go. You also discover that bad experiences always pass. Under the breath's gentle tuition you learn to stop living in a fairytale world in which everything stays magically the same and you can hold on to things and people for ever. You cannot finally hold on to anything, just as you cannot inhale and hold your breath indefinitely. The breath teaches you about the process of life, of gathering in and giving out, of giving up the old in order to make space for the new, just as the stale air is expelled to allow a tide of fresh air and energy to flow in.

the breath registers everything
As time goes on, you come to see what a fantastic and subtle mechanism the breath is. It is like a musical instrument, which can play anything from the softest, subtlest, tenderest notes, up to a thunderous crescendo. It registers everything, reflects everything, because it is affected by everything. Each emotion, each subtle thought, brings about a new pattern in the breathing. As you become more skilled

in tuning into it, the breath becomes a diagnostic tool, making you aware of all kinds of subtleties in your experience.

You may be following the breath when at a certain moment a mental picture of an old friend drifts across your mind. You then notice that the breath has become slightly shallower and more constricted. Why is that? You may at first assume that your mind has become less concentrated, that some of your energy has left the breathing to engage with the thought of your friend, and that this accounts for the slight lack of smoothness in the breath. But then, exploring your experience more deeply, you sense that the tightness in the breath reflects some anxiety in relation to your friend. What is that about? You may realize that you are concerned for him or her, that something in you feels intuitively that a recent decision they have taken may not be right. The tightening of your breath was in response to a subtle anticipation that your friend was doing something that could make them unhappy. The breath registered the tightening in your body against the pain of a friend potentially in trouble.

In fact, the breath as an instrument does not just register what is happening internally; it also responds to external conditions: temperature, atmospheric pressure, wind, sunlight, the solidity of the ground. If any of these were different then the breath would be different. As you explore this idea more and more, you begin to see that the breath is the product of a tremendous range of conditions.

Through the breath you can have a moment by moment demonstration of one of the key insights of Buddhism: that everything depends upon conditions. You can watch the in-breath building like a wave, as all kinds of factors come together to support it. Then you can watch it die away as those conditions change.

More than this, by reflecting on what is happening, you can glimpse something of a vision of inter-connectedness. You can see the universe as a vast field of phenomena, arising in dependence on conditions, moment by moment, in which every phenomenon conditions all the others. Seen in the light of this vision, the breath is the product of an endless, inconceivable array of conditions. Similarly, the movement of the breath in our body plays its part in conditioning everything around it. In this way we can watch the dance of life unfolding moment by moment, with everything affecting, and being affected by, everything else.

integrity of practice

Although I originally imagined that learning to focus on the breath would be mainly about relaxation and concentration, the meditation actually goes much deeper than this. It provides an education for your heart, schooling you to become a genuine, authentic human being. This is because it brings you close to your living experience rather than all your ideas and fantasies about it. It also teaches you to make a sincere, steady effort, moment by moment, day by day, year by year.

The practice humbles those who adopt a macho, 'I always count to ten,' attitude to it. To those who suffer from self-doubt it gives strength and determination. In fact, the qualities that are needed to merge your awareness with the breath are the same ones that are needed to be an authentic human being: honesty with yourself, clarity, kindness and sensitivity, determination and perseverance.

As meditation is a direct encounter with yourself, it brings self-knowledge. The simple act of paying attention to one thing brings up all kinds of emotions, questions, and ideas, just as one small candle can throw large shadows across a room. You see yourself at your best and at your worst. But whatever comes up you keep turning back to the breath. This gives you the ability to experience all kinds of different mental states, including very strong emotions, without being carried away by them.

The people I know who have gone most deeply into meditation are not spaced-out specimens inhabiting some stratosphere of the mind. They are deeply human, able to empathize with all kinds of people, because they have experienced their own human emotions at full strength. Yet I also experience them as more than human, because they are not carried away by their emotions as most people are. They maintain a steady stream of kindness, and in themselves they are happy, relaxed, and light-hearted. Everything they do has a quality of naturalness. They are just being themselves – not in a self-indulgent way, but authentic and sincere.

When I first learned to meditate I was looking for miracles and supernormal mental states. These days I just want to be like these men and women, who have faithfully practised meditation for half a lifetime or more. Their genuineness, love, and authenticity are the greatest miracle I could hope to see.

This practice of paying attention to the breath may be very simple, but we should not let that deceive us. It deserves our greatest respect. If we keep turning our attention, again and again and again, to this fundamental experience of being alive, of taking in air and returning it to the universe, we shall find deepening satisfaction within it. We shall find that it is teaching us how to live with integrity, to become authentic human beings. We shall find that it is taking us on an endless voyage of discovery.

further reading

Change Your Mind: A Practical Guide to Buddhist Meditation, by Paramananda, Windhorse Publications, Birmingham, 1996.
Introduces meditation on the breath and on positive emotion, and then explores intention, balanced effort, and other topics touched on in this book, but in more detail and with a poetic lightness.

Wildmind: A Step-by-Step Guide to Meditation, by Bodhipaksa, Windhorse Publications, Birmingham, 2003.
Based on the very popular *Wildmind* meditation teaching website, this book offers a practical and clear approach to meditation on the breath.

Meditation: The Buddhist Way of Tranquillity and Insight, by Kamalashila, Windhorse Publications, Birmingham, 1999.
A very useful and systematic introduction to Buddhist meditation, with very good sections on meditation posture and on mindfulness of breathing.

Sitting, by Kamalashila, Windhorse Publications, Birmingham, 1988.
This is based on the posture section from Kamalashila's book on meditation.

Breath by Breath: The Liberating Practice of Insight Meditation, by Larry Rosenberg, Shambhala Publications, Boston MA, 1998 and Thorsons, London, 1999.
An excellent introduction to the sixteen contemplations of the *Ānāpānasati Sutta*, full of stories and helpful advice, with an English translation of the text.

Mindfulness with Breathing: A Manual for Serious Beginners, by Buddhadasa Bhikkhu, Wisdom Publications, Somerville MA, 1997.
Covers the same ground as Larry Rosenberg's book, but from a more traditional viewpoint. Buddhadasa Bhikkhu was a very influential Thai meditation teacher.

Free Your Breath, Free Your Life, by Dennis Lewis, Shambhala Publications, Boston MA, 2004.
Not mainly about meditation, this is a book about breathing and how to learn to breathe in a natural way free of tensions. It is full of practical exercises.

The windhorse symbolizes the energy of the Enlightened mind carrying the truth of the Buddha's teachings to all corners of the world. On its back the windhorse bears three jewels: a brilliant gold jewel represents the Buddha, the ideal of Enlightenment, a sparkling blue jewel represents the teachings of the Buddha, the Dharma, and a glowing red jewel, the community of the Buddha's enlightened followers, the Sangha. Windhorse Publications, through the medium of books, similarly takes these three jewels out to the world.

Windhorse Publications is a Buddhist publishing house, staffed by practising Buddhists. We place great emphasis on producing books of high quality, accessible and relevant to those interested in Buddhism at whatever level. Drawing on the whole range of the Buddhist tradition, our books include translations of traditional texts, commentaries, books that make links with Western culture and ways of life, biographies of Buddhists, and works on meditation.

As a charitable institution we welcome donations to help us continue our work. We also welcome manuscripts on aspects of Buddhism or meditation. For orders and catalogues log on to www.windhorsepublications.com or contact:

Windhorse Publications	Consortium	Windhorse Books
11 Park Road	1045 Westgate Drive	P O Box 574
Birmingham	St Paul MN 55114	Newtown NSW 2042
B13 8AB	USA	Australia
UK		

Windhorse Publications is an arm of the Friends of the Western Buddhist Order, which has more than sixty centres on four continents. Through these centres, members of the Western Buddhist Order offer regular programmes of events for the general public and for more experienced students. These include meditation classes, public talks, study on Buddhist themes and texts, and bodywork classes such as t'ai chi, yoga, and massage. The FWBO also runs several retreat centres and the Karuna Trust, a fundraising charity that supports social welfare projects in the slums and villages of India.

Many FWBO centres have residential spiritual communities and ethical businesses associated with them. Arts activities are encouraged too, as is the development of strong bonds of friendship between people who share the same ideals. In this way the FWBO is developing a unique approach to Buddhism, not simply as a set of techniques, but as a creatively directed way of life for people living in the modern world.

If you would like more information about the FWBO please visit the website at www.fwbo.org or write to:

London Buddhist Centre	Aryaloka	Sydney Buddhist Centre
51 Roman Road	14 Heartwood Circle	24 Enmore Road
London	Newmarket NH 03857	Sydney NSW 2042
E2 0HU	USA	Australia
UK		

ALSO FROM WINDHORSE PUBLICATIONS

WILDMIND: A STEP-BY-STEP GUIDE TO MEDITATION

BODHIPAKSA

A Wildmind is as spacious as a clear blue sky, as still as a lake at dawn; such a mind is a source of richness and fulfilment. It is a mind that is free, spontaeous, and abundantly creative. It is a place we can spend the rest of our lives exploring.

Buddhist meditation teacher Bodhipaksa shows us how we can use simple meditation practices to realize the potential of our minds and hearts, freeing ourselves from restrictive habits and fears and developing a more loving heart and a clearer mind. Drawn from the very successful online meditation website, www.wildmind.org, it is written in short sections to encourage reflection and for practices to 'sink in'.

256 pages, with photographs
ISBN 1 899579 55 9
£11.99/$18.95/€18.95

CHANGE YOUR MIND:
A PRACTICAL GUIDE TO BUDDHIST MEDITATION

PARAMANANDA

Buddhism is based on the truth that, with effort, we can change the way we are. But how? Among the many methods Buddhism has to offer, meditation is the most direct. It is the art of getting to know one's own mind and learning to encourage what is best in us.

This bestseller is an approachable and thorough guide to meditation, based on traditional material but written in a light and modern style. Colourfully illustrated with anecdotes and tips from the author's experience as a meditator and teacher, it also offers refreshing inspiration to seasoned meditators.

208 pages, with photographs
ISBN 0 904766 81 0
£8.99/$17.95/€17.95

INTRODUCING BUDDHISM

CHRIS PAULING

Introducing Buddhism is a lively and engaging guide for Westerners who want to learn more about Buddhism as a path of spiritual growth.

Written in a clear, informal style, it explains the essential teachings and practices on which all mainstream Buddhists can agree, and shows how this ancient wisdom is more than ever relevant to the psychological, social, and spiritual issues concerning men and women in the modern West.

80 pages
ISBN 0 904766 97 7
£4.99/$8.95/€8.95

THE BUDDHIST PATH TO AWAKENING

TEJANANDA

The word Buddha means 'one who is awake'. In this accessible introduction, Tejananda alerts us to the Buddha's wake-up call, illustrating how the Buddhist path can help us develop a clearer mind and a more compassionate heart.

Covering the Four Noble Truths, the Threefold Path, the Three Jewels, and much more, Tejananda gives us a straightforward and encouraging description of the path of the Buddha and his followers – one that leads each of us to our own awakening.

224 pages, with diagrams
ISBN 1 899579 02 8
£8.99/$17.95/€17.95